The French Historical Revolution

Key Contemporary Thinkers

The French Historical Revolution
The *Annales* School, 1929–89

Peter Burke

Stanford University Press
Stanford, California
1990

Stanford University Press
Stanford, California
© 1990 Peter Burke
Originating publisher: Polity Press, Cambridge
  in association with Basil Blackwell, Oxford
First published in the U.S.A. by
  Stanford University Press, 1990
Printed in Great Britain
Cloth ISBN 0-8047-1836-9
Paper ISBN 0-8047-1837-7
LC 90-70699
This book is printed on acid-free paper

Contents

Acknowledgements

It goes without saying that this study owes a good deal to conversations with members of the *Annales* group, notably with Fernand Braudel, Emmanuel Le Roy Ladurie, Jacques Le Goff, Michel Vovelle, Krzysztof Pomian, Roger Chartier, and Jacques Revel, in Paris and also in more exotic locations, from the Taj Mahal to Emmanuel College.

I should like to thank my wife, Maria Lúcia, my publisher, John Thompson, and Roger Chartier, for their comments on an earlier draft of this study. I am also indebted to Juan Maiguashca, who fired my enthusiasm for *Annales*, some thirty years ago, and to dialogues with Alan Baker, Norman Birnbaum, John Bossy, Stuart Clark, Robert Darnton, Clifford Davies, Natalie Davis, Javier Gil Pujol, Carlo Ginzburg, Ranajit Guha, Eric Hobsbawm, Gábor Klaniczay, Geoffrey Parker, Gwyn Prins, Carlos Martínez Shaw, Ivo Schöffer, Henk Wesseling, and others who have, like myself, tried to combine their involvement with *Annales* with a measure of detachment from it.

Introduction

A remarkable amount of the most innovative, the most memorable and the most significant historical writing of the twentieth century has been produced in France. *La nouvelle histoire*, as it is sometimes called, is at least as famous, as French, and as controversial as *la nouvelle cuisine*.[1] A good deal of this new history is the work of a particular group associated with the journal founded in 1929, and most conveniently known as *Annales*.[2] Outsiders generally call this group the '*Annales* school', emphasizing what they have in common, while insiders often deny the existence of such a school, emphasizing individual approaches within the group.[3]

At the centre of the group are Lucien Febvre, Marc Bloch, Fernand Braudel, Georges Duby, Jacques Le Goff, and Emmanuel Le Roy Ladurie. Nearer the edge are Ernest Labrousse, Pierre Vilar, Maurice Agulhon and Michel Vovelle, four distinguished historians whose commitment to a Marxist approach to history – particularly strong in Vilar's case – places them outside the inner circle. On or beyond the fringe are Roland Mousnier and Michel Foucault, who make brief appearances in this study because of the overlap between their historical interests and those associated with *Annales*.

The journal, which is now more than sixty years old, was founded in order to promote a new kind of history, and it continues to encourage innovation. The leading ideas behind

Annales might be summarized briefly as follows. In the first place, the substitution of a problem-oriented analytical history for a traditional narrative of events. In the second place, the history of the whole range of human activities in the place of a mainly political history. In the third place – in order to achieve the first two aims – a collaboration with other disciplines: with geography, sociology, psychology, economics, linguistics, social anthropology, and so on. As Febvre put it, with his character-istic use of the imperative, 'Historians, be geographers. Be jurists too, and sociologists, and psychologists'.[4] He was always on the alert 'to break down compartments' (*abattre les cloisons*) and to fight narrow specialization, '*l'esprit de spécialité*'.[5] In a similar way, Braudel wrote his *Mediterranean* in the way he did in order to 'prove that history can do more than study walled gardens'.[6]

The aim of this book is to describe, to analyse, and to evaluate the achievement of the *Annales* school. This school is often perceived from outside as a monolithic group with a uniform historical practice, quantitative in method, determinist in its assumptions, and hostile, or at best indifferent, to politics and to events. This stereotype of the *Annales* school ignores divergences between individual members of the group and also developments over time. It might be better to speak not of a 'school', but of the *Annales* movement.[7]

This movement may be divided into three phases. In the first phase, from the 1920s to 1945, it was small, radical and subver-sive, fighting a guerrilla action against traditional history, politi-cal history, and the history of events. After the Second World War, the rebels took over the historical Establishment. This sec-ond phase of the movement, in which it was most truly a 'school' with distinctive concepts (notably '*structure*' and '*conjoncture*') and distinctive methods (notably the 'serial history' of changes over the long term), was dominated by Fernand Braudel.

A third phase in the history of the movement opened around the year 1968. It is marked by fragmentation (*émiettement*). By this time, the influence of the movement – especially in France – was so great that it had lost much of its former distinctiveness. It was a unified 'school' only in the eyes of its foreign admirers and its domestic critics, who continued to reproach it for underestimating the importance of politics and of the history of events. In the last twenty years, some members of the group have turned from socio-economic to socio-cultural history, while others are rediscovering political history and even narrative.

The history of *Annales* may thus be interpreted in terms of the succession of three generations. It also illustrates the common cyclical process by which the rebels of today turn into the Establishment of tomorrow, and are in turn rebelled against. All the same, some major concerns have persisted. Indeed, the journal and the individuals associated with it offer the most sustained example of fruitful interaction between history and the social sciences to be found in our century. It is for this reason that I have chosen to write about them.

This brief survey of the *Annales* movement attempts to cross several cultural boundaries. It attempts to explain the French to the English-speaking world, the 1920s to a later generation, and the practice of historians to sociologists, anthropologists, geographers, and others. My account is itself presented in the form of a history, and attempts to combine a chronological with a thematic organization.

The problem with such a combination, here as elsewhere in history, is what has been called 'the contemporaneity of the non-contemporary'. Braudel, for example, although he was exceptionally open to new ideas, even late in his long life, did not fundamentally change his way of looking at history or indeed of writing history from the 1930s, when he was planning his *Mediterranean*, to the 1980s, when he was working on his book on France. For this reason it has proved necessary to take some liberties with chronological order.

This book is at once something less and something more than a study in intellectual history. It does not aspire to be the definitive scholarly study of the *Annales* movement that I hope someone will write in the twenty-first century. Such a study will have to make use of sources I have not seen (such as the manuscript drafts of Marc Bloch or the unpublished letters of Febvre and Braudel).[8] Its author will need a specialized knowledge not only of the history of historical writing, but also of the history of twentieth-century France.

What I have tried to write is rather different. It is a more personal essay. I have sometimes described myself as a 'fellow-traveller' of *Annales* – in other words, an outsider who has (like many other foreign historians) been inspired by the movement. I have followed its fortunes fairly closely in the last thirty years. All the same, Cambridge is sufficiently distant from Paris to make it possible to write a critical history of the *Annales* achievement.

Although Febvre and Braudel were both formidable academic politicians, little will be said in the pages that follow about this aspect of the movement – the rivalry between the Sorbonne and the Hautes Etudes, for example, or the struggle for power over appointments and curricula.[9] I have also, with some regret, resisted the temptation to write an ethnographic study of the inhabitants of 54 Boulevard Raspail – their ancestors, intermarriages, factions, patron–client networks, styles of life, mentalities, and so on.

Instead, I shall concentrate on the major books produced by members of the group, and attempt to assess their importance in the history of historical writing. It sounds paradoxical to discuss a movement that has been held together by a journal in terms of books rather than articles.[10] However, it is a cluster of monographs that has made the greatest impact (on professionals and the general public alike) over the long term.

The movement has too often been discussed as if it could be equated with three or four people. The achievements of Lucien Febvre, Marc Bloch, Fernand Braudel and others are indeed spectacular. However, as in the case of many intellectual movements, this one is a collective enterprise to which significant contributions have been made by a number of individuals. This point is most obvious in the case of the third generation, but it is also true for the age of Braudel and for that of the founders. Team-work had been a dream of Lucien Febvre's, as early as 1936.[11] After the war, it became a reality. Collaborative projects on French history have included the history of the social structure, the history of agricultural productivity, the history of the eighteenth-century book, the history of education, the history of housing, and a computer-based study of conscripts in the nineteenth century.

This study ends with a discussion of responses to *Annales*, whether enthusiastic or critical, an account of its reception in different parts of the world and in different disciplines, and an attempt to place it in the history of historical writing. My aim (despite the relative brevity of this book) is to allow the reader to see the movement as a whole.

1

The Old Historiographical Regime and its Critics

Lucien Febvre and Marc Bloch were the leaders of what might be called the French Historical Revolution. In order to interpret the actions of revolutionaries, however, it is necessary to know something of the old regime which they wish to overturn. To understand as well as to describe this regime, we cannot confine ourselves to the situation in France around 1900, when Febvre and Bloch were students. We need to examine the history of historical writing over the long term.

Since the age of Herodotus and Thucydides, history has been written in the West in a variety of genres – the monastic chronicle, the political memoir, the antiquarian treatise, and so on. However, the dominant form has long been the narrative of political and military events, presented as the story of the great deeds of great men – the captains and the kings. This dominant form was first seriously challenged during the Enlightenment.[1]

At this time, around the middle of the eighteenth century, a number of writers and scholars in Scotland, France, Italy, Germany, and elsewhere began to concern themselves with what they called the 'history of society', a history that would not be confined to war and politics, but would include laws and trade, morals, and the 'manners' that were the centre of attention in Voltaire's famous *Essai sur les moeurs*.

These scholars dismissed what John Millar of Glasgow once called 'that common surface of events which occupies the details of the vulgar historian' in order to concentrate on the history of structures such as the feudal system or the British constitution. Some of them were concerned with the reconstruction of past attitudes and values, notably with the history of the value-system known as 'chivalry', others with the history of art, literature, and music. By the end of the century, this international group of scholars had produced an extremely important body of work. Some historians, notably Edward Gibbon in his *Decline and Fall of the Roman Empire*, integrated this new socio-cultural history into a narrative of political events.

However, one of the consequences of the so-called 'Copernican Revolution' in history associated with Leopold von Ranke was to marginalize, or remarginalize, social and cultural history. Ranke's own interests were not limited to political history. He wrote on the Reformation and the Counter-Reformation, and he did not reject the history of society, art, literature, or science. All the same, the movement Ranke led and the new historical paradigm he formulated undermined the 'new history' of the eighteenth century. His emphasis on archive sources made the historians who worked on social and cultural history look mere *dilettanti*.

Ranke's followers were more narrow-minded than the master himself, and in an age when historians were aspiring to become professionals, non-political history was excluded from the new academic discipline.[2] The new professional journals founded in the later nineteenth century, such as the *Historische Zeitschrift* (founded 1856), the *Revue Historique* (1876) and the *English Historical Review* (1886), concentrated on the history of political events (the preface to the first volume of the *English Historical Review* declared its intent to concentrate on 'States and politics'). The ideals of the new professional historians were articulated in a number of treatises on historical method, such as the *Introduction aux études historiques* (1897) by the French historians Langlois and Seignebos.

Dissenting voices could of course be heard in the nineteenth century. Michelet and Burckhardt, who produced their histories of the Renaissance more or less at the same moment, in 1855 and

1860 respectively, had much wider views of history than the Rankeans. Burckhardt viewed history as the field of interaction of three forces – the state, religion and culture – while Michelet called for what we would now describe as 'history from below'; in his own words, 'the history of those who have suffered, worked, declined and died without being able to describe their sufferings'.[3]

Again, the masterpiece of the French ancient historian Fustel de Coulanges, *The Ancient City* (1864), concentrated on the history of religion, the family and morality rather than on politics or events. Marx too offered an alternative historical paradigm to that of Ranke. According to Marx's view of history, the fundamental causes of change were to be found in the tensions within social and economic structures.

The economic historians were perhaps the best organized of the dissenters from political history. Gustav Schmoller, for example, professor at Strasbourg (or rather Strassburg, because at that time it was still part of Germany) from 1872, was the leader of an important historical school. A journal of social and economic history, the *Vierteljahrsschrift für Sozial und Wirtschaftsgeschichte*, was founded in 1893. In Britain, classic studies of economic history, such as William Cunningham's *Growth of English Trade* and J. E. Thorold Rogers's *Six Centuries of Work and Wages*, go back to 1882 and 1884 respectively.[4] In France, Henri Hauser, Henri Sée and Paul Mantoux were all beginning to write on economic history at the end of the nineteenth century.[5]

By the later nineteenth century, the dominance, or as Schmoller put it, the 'imperialism', of political history was frequently challenged. J. R. Green, for example, opened his *Short History of the English People* (1874) with the bold claim to have 'devoted more space to Chaucer than to Cressy, to Caxton than to the petty strife of Yorkist and Lancastrian, to the Poor Law of Elizabeth than to her victory at Cadiz, to the Methodist Revival than to the escape of the Young Pretender'.[6]

The founders of the new discipline of sociology expressed similar views. Auguste Comte, for example, made fun of what he called the 'petty details childishly studied by the irrational curiosity of blind compilers of useless anecdotes', and advocated what he called, in a famous phrase, 'history without names'.[7] Herbert Spencer complained that, 'The biographies of monarchs (and our children learn little else) throw scarcely any light upon the science of society.'[8] In similar fashion, Emile Durkheim dismissed specific events (*événements particuliers*) as no more than 'superficial manifestations', the apparent rather than the real history of a given nation.[9]

In the years around 1900, criticisms of political history were particularly sharp, and suggestions for its replacement were particularly fertile.[10] In Germany, these were the years of the so-called 'Lamprecht controversy'. Karl Lamprecht, a professor at Leipzig, contrasted political history, which was merely the history of individuals, with cultural or economic history, which was the history of the people. He later defined history as 'primarily a socio-psychological science'.[11]

In the United States, Frederick Jackson Turner's famous study of 'the significance of the frontier in American history' (1893) made a clear break with the history of political events, while early in the new century a movement was launched by James Harvey Robinson under the slogan of the 'New History'. According to Robinson, 'History includes every trace and vestige of everything that man has done or thought since first he appeared on the earth.' As for method, 'The New History will avail itself of all those discoveries that are being made about mankind by anthropologists, economists, psychologists and sociologists.'[12]

In France too around the year 1900, the nature of history was the subject of a lively debate. The narrow-mindedness of the historical Establishment should not be exaggerated. The founder of the *Revue Historique*, Gabriel Monod, combined his enthusiasm for German 'scientific' history with an admiration for Michelet (whom he knew personally and whose biography he wrote), and was himself admired by his pupils Hauser and Febvre.

Again, Ernest Lavisse, one of the most important historians active in France at this time, was the general editor of a history of France which appeared in ten volumes between 1900 and

1912. His own interests were primarily in political history, from Frederick the Great to Louis XIV. However, the conception of history revealed by these ten volumes was a broad one. The introductory section was written by a geographer, and the volume on the Renaissance penned by a cultural historian, while Lavisse's own account of the age of Louis XIV devoted a substantial amount of space to the arts, and in particular to the politics of culture.[13] In other words, it is inexact to think of the established professional historians of the period as exclusively concerned with the narrative of political events.

All the same, historians were still perceived by the social scientists in precisely this way. Durkheim's dismissal of events has already been quoted. His follower, the economist François Simiand, went still further in this direction in a famous article attacking what he called the 'idols of the tribe of historians'. According to Simiand, there were three idols which must be toppled. There was the 'political idol' – 'the perpetual preoccupation with political history, political facts, wars etc., which gives these events an exaggerated importance'. There was the 'individual idol' – in other words, the overemphasis on so-called great men, so that even studies of institutions were presented in the form 'Pontchartrain and the Parlement of Paris', and so on. Finally, there was the 'chronological idol', that is, 'the habit of losing oneself in studies of origins'.[14]

All three themes would be dear to *Annales*, and we shall return to them. The attack on the idols of the historians' tribe made particular reference to one of the tribal chieftains, Lavisse's protégé Charles Seignebos, professor at the Sorbonne and co-author of a well-known introduction to the study of history.[15] It was perhaps for this reason that Seignebos became the symbol of everything the reformers opposed. In fact, he was not an exclusively political historian, but also wrote on civilization. He was interested in the relation between history and the social sciences, though he did not have the same view of this relation as Simiand or Febvre, who both published sharp criticisms of his work. Simiand's critique appeared in a new journal, the *Revue de Synthèse Historique*, founded in 1900 by a great intellectual entrepreneur,

Henri Berr, in order to encourage historians to collaborate with other disciplines, particularly psychology and sociology, in the hope of producing what Berr called a 'historical' or 'collective' psychology.[16] In other words, what the Americans call 'psycho-history' goes back considerably further than the 1950s and Erik Erikson's famous study of *Young Man Luther*.[17]

Berr's ideal of a historical psychology to be achieved by interdisciplinary co-operation had a great appeal for two younger men who wrote for his journal. Their names were Lucien Febvre and Marc Bloch.

2

The Founders: Lucien Febvre and Marc Bloch

In its first generation, the *Annales* movement had two leaders, not one: Lucien Febvre, a specialist on the sixteenth century, and the medievalist Marc Bloch. Their approaches to history were remarkably similar, but they were very different in temperament. Febvre, the elder by eight years, was expansive, vehement and combative, with a tendency to scold his colleagues if they did not do what he wanted, while Bloch was serene, ironic, and laconic, with an almost English love of qualifications and understatements.[1] Despite or because of these differences, the two men worked together very well during the twenty years between the wars.[2]

I   THE EARLY YEARS

Lucien Febvre entered the Ecole Normale Supérieure in 1897. At this time, the Ecole was quite separate from the University of Paris. It was a small but intellectually high-powered college, which has been called 'the French equivalent of Jowett's Balliol'.[3] It accepted fewer than forty students a year, and was organized on the lines of a traditional British public school (the students were all boarders and discipline was strict).[4] The teaching was by seminar not lecture, and the seminars were given by leading scholars in different disciplines. Febvre was apparently 'allergic' to the philosopher Henri Bergson, but he learned a great deal from four of Bergson's colleagues.[5]

The first of these was Paul Vidal de la Blache, a geographer who was interested in collaborating with historians and sociologists, and had founded a new journal, the *Annales de Géographie* (1891) to encourage this approach.[6] The second of these teachers at the Ecole was the philosopher–anthropologist Lucien Lévy-Bruhl, much of whose work was concerned with what he called 'pre-logical thought' or 'primitive mentality', a theme that would surface in Febvre's work in the 1930s. The third was the art historian Emile Mâle, one of the first to concentrate not on the history of forms, but on the history of images – 'iconography', as it is generally called today. His famous study of religious art of the thirteenth century was published in 1898, the very year Febvre entered the Ecole. Finally, there was the linguist Antoine Meillet, a student of Durkheim's who was particularly interested in the social aspects of language. Febvre's admiration for Meillet and his interest in the social history of language is apparent in a series of reviews of books by linguists which he wrote between 1906 and 1926 for Henri Berr's *Revue de Synthèse Historique*.[7]

Febvre also acknowledged debts to earlier historians. He was a lifelong admirer of the work of Michelet. He recognized Burckhardt as one of his 'masters', together with the art historian Louis Courajod. He also confessed to a more surprising influence on his work, that of the *Histoire socialiste de la révolution française* (1901–3), by the Left-wing politician Jean Jaurès, 'so rich in economic and social intuitions'.[8]

The influence of Jaurès can be seen in Febvre's doctoral thesis. Febvre chose to study his own region, Franche-Comté, the area around Besançon, in the later sixteenth century, when it was ruled by Philip II of Spain. The title of the thesis, 'Philippe II et la Franche-Comté', masks the fact that the study itself was an important contribution to social and cultural as well as to political history. It was concerned not only with the Revolt of the Netherlands and the rise of absolutism, but also with the 'fierce struggle between two rival classes', the declining nobility, who were going into debt, and the rising bourgeoisie of merchants and lawyers, who were buying up their estates. This schema looks Marxist – but Febvre differed sharply from Marx in describing the struggle between the two groups as 'no mere economic conflict but a conflict of ideas and feelings as well'.[9] His interpretation of this conflict, indeed of history in general, was not unlike that of Jaurès, who claimed to be 'at once materialist with Marx and mystical with Michelet', reconciling social forces with individual passions.[10]

Another arresting and influential feature of Febvre's study was its geographical introduction, outlining the distinctive contours of the region. The geographical introduction which was almost *de rigueur* in the provincial monographs of the *Annales* school in the 1960s may have been modelled on Braudel's famous *Mediterranean*, but did not originate with him.

Febvre was sufficiently interested in historical geography to publish (at the instigation of Henri Berr, the editor of the *Revue de Synthèse Historique*) a general study of the topic under the title *La terre et l'évolution humaine*. This study had been planned before the First World War, but it was interrupted when the author switched roles from university teacher to captain of a company of machine-gunners. After the war, Febvre went back to work on this study, with the help of a collaborator. It was published in 1922.

This wide-ranging essay, which annoyed some professional geographers because it was the work of an outsider, was a development of the ideas of Febvre's old teacher Vidal de la Blache. Important for Febvre in a rather different way was the German geographer Ratzel. Febvre was a kind of intellectual oyster, who produced his own ideas most easily when irritated by the conclusions of a colleague. Ratzel was another pioneer of human geography (*Anthropogéographie*, as he called it), but unlike Vidal de la Blache he stressed the influence of the physical environment on human destiny.[11]

In this debate between geographical determinism and human liberty, Febvre warmly supported Vidal and attacked Ratzel, stressing the variety of possible responses to the challenge of a given environment. For him there were no necessities, only possibilities (*Des nécessités, nulle part. Des possibilités, partout*).[12] A river – to quote one of Febvre's favourite examples – might be treated by one society as a barrier, yet as a route by another. In the last analysis, it was not the physical environment that determined this collective choice, but men, their way of life, and their attitudes. Religious attitudes were included. In a discussion of rivers and roads, Febvre did not forget to discuss pilgrimage routes.[13]

Bloch's career was not very different from Febvre's. He too attended the Ecole Normale, where his father Gustave taught ancient history. He too learned from Meillet and Lévy-Bruhl. However, as the discussion of his later works will argue, he owed most to the sociologist Emile Durkheim, who began to teach at the Ecole at about the time Bloch arrived. An old Ecole man himself, Durkheim had learned from his studies with Fustel de Coulanges to take history seriously.[14] In later life, Bloch acknowledged his profound debt to Durkheim's journal the *Année Sociologique*, which was read with enthusiasm by a number of historians of his generation, such as the classicist Louis Gernet and the sinologist Marcel Granet.[15]

Despite his interest in contemporary politics, Bloch chose to specialize in the Middle Ages. Like Febvre, he was interested in historical geography, his speciality being the Ile-de-France, on which he published a study in 1913. The study of the Ile-de-France shows that, again like Febvre, Bloch was thinking in a problem-oriented way. In a regional study he went so far as to call into question the very notion of a region, arguing that it depended on the problem with which one was concerned. 'Why', he wrote, 'should one expect the jurist who is interested in feudalism, the economist who is studying the evolution of property in the countryside in modern times, and the philologist who is working on popular dialects, all to stop at precisely identical frontiers?'[16]

Bloch's commitment to geography was less than Febvre's, while his commitment to sociology was greater. However, both men were thinking in an interdisciplinary way. Bloch, for example, stressed the need for the local historian to combine the skills of an archaeologist, a palaeographer, a historian of law and so on.[17] The two men obviously needed to meet each other. The opportunity was provided by their appointments to posts at the University of Strasbourg.

II STRASBOURG

The Milieu   The Strasbourg period of daily meetings between Bloch and Febvre lasted only thirteen years, from 1920 to 1933, but it was crucially important for the *Annales* movement. Its importance was all the greater because the two men were surrounded by an extremely lively interdisciplinary group.

It is also worth emphasizing the milieu in which this group came together. Strasbourg in the years following the First World War was effectively a new university, since the city had just been reclaimed from Germany. The milieu favoured intellectual innovation and facilitated the exchange of ideas across disciplinary frontiers.[18]

When Febvre and Bloch met in 1920, soon after their appointments as professor and *maître de conférences* respectively, their acquaintance rapidly ripened into friendship.[19] Their offices were adjoining, and the doors were left open.[20] Their unending discussions were sometimes shared with colleagues such as the social psychologist Charles Blondel, whose ideas were important for Febvre, and the sociologist Maurice Halbwachs, whose study of the social framework of memory, published in 1925, made a deep impression on Bloch.[21]

A number of other members of the Strasbourg faculty shared or came to share interests with Febvre and Bloch. Henri Bremond, the author of the monumental *Histoire littéraire du sentiment religieux en France depuis la fin des guerres de religion* (1916–24), lectured at Strasbourg in 1923. Bremond's concern with historical psychology was an inspiration to Febvre in his own work on the Reformation.[22] Georges Lefebvre, the historian of the French Revolution, whose concern with the history of mentalities was close to that of the founders of *Annales*, taught at Strasbourg from 1928 till 1937. It does not seem fanciful to suggest that the idea of Lefebvre's famous study of 'the great fear of 1789' owes something to an earlier study of rumour by Marc Bloch.[23] Gabriel Le Bras, a pioneer in the historical sociology of religion, also taught at Strasbourg. So did the ancient historian André Piganiol, whose study of the Roman games, published in 1923, reveals an interest in anthropology, like a study of Bloch's published a year later – *The Royal Touch*.[24]

The Royal Touch has a strong claim to be regarded as one of the great historical works of our century.[25] It is concerned with the belief, current in England and France from the Middle Ages to the eighteenth century, that kings had the power to cure scrofula, a skin disease known as 'the king's evil', by the power of the royal touch, and with the ritual of touching the sick for this purpose.

The subject may still seem somewhat marginal, and certainly did so in the 1920s – Bloch makes an ironic reference to an English colleague who commented on 'this curious by-path of yours'.[26] For Bloch, on the contrary, the royal touch was not a by-path at all but a main road, indeed *une voie royale* in every sense. It was a case study that illuminated major problems. The author claimed with some justification that his book was a contribution to the political history of Europe in the true, broad sense of the term 'political' (*au sens large, au vrai sens du mot*), because the book was concerned with ideas of kingship. 'The royal miracle was above all the expression of a particular conception of supreme political power.'[27]

The Royal Touch   *The Royal Touch* was remarkable in at least three other respects. In the first place, because it was not confined to a conventional historical period like the Middle Ages. Following the advice he would later formulate in general terms in *The Historian's Craft*, Bloch chose the period to fit the problem, which meant he had to write what Braudel, a generation later, would call 'the history of the long-term'. This long-term perspective led Bloch to some interesting conclusions, notably that the ritual of touching did not merely survive into the seventeenth century, the age of Descartes and Louis XIV, but flourished as never before, at least in the sense that Louis XIV touched greater numbers of sufferers than his predecessors. It was no mere 'fossil'.[28]

In the second place, the book was a contribution to what Bloch called 'religious psychology'. The study was centrally concerned with the history of miracles, and it concluded with an explicit discussion of the problem of explaining how people could possibly believe in such 'collective illusions'.[29] Bloch noted that some sufferers came back to be touched a second time, which suggests that they knew the treatment had not worked, but that this had not undermined their faith. 'It was the expectation of the miracle which created faith in it' (*Ce qui créa la foi au miracle, ce fut l'idée qu'il devait y avoir un miracle*).[30] In the famous phrase of the philosopher Karl Popper, formulated a few years later, the belief was not 'falsifiable'.[31]

This discussion of the psychology of belief was not the sort of thing one expected to find in the 1920s in a historical study. This was the business of psychologists, sociologists, or anthropologists. In fact, Bloch did discuss his book with a psychologist, his Strasbourg colleague Charles Blondel, as well as with Febvre.[32] Bloch was also aware of the work of James Frazer, and of what *The Golden Bough* had to say about sacred kingship, just as he was aware of what Lucien Lévy-Bruhl had to say about 'primitive mentality'.[33] Although Bloch did not make frequent use of that term, his book was a pioneer contribution to what we now call the history of 'mentalities'. It might also be described as an essay in historical sociology, or historical anthropology, focusing on belief systems and the sociology of knowledge.

The phrase Bloch did use more than once to describe his book was 'collective representations' (*représentations collectives*), a phrase closely associated with the sociologist Emile Durkheim, like the phrase 'social facts' (*faits sociaux*), which can also be found in Bloch's pages.[34] Indeed, his whole approach owed a good deal to that of Durkheim and his school.[35] In one respect at least, it might be criticized with hindsight as somewhat too Durkheimian.

Although Bloch is careful to record doubts about the royal touch expressed during the long period covered by his book, he still creates too strong an impression of consensus, perhaps because he does not offer any systematic discussion of the kinds of people who believed (or on occasion disbelieved), or of the groups in whose interest it was that other people should believe in the royal touch. He does not discuss the phenomenon in terms of ideology. Of course, in Bloch's day the concept 'ideology' tended to be used in a crude, reductionist way. This is no longer the case, and it is difficult to imagine a historian associated with *Annales*, Georges Duby for example, discussing the royal touch today without recourse to this concept.

A third feature that makes Bloch's study important is its concern with what the author called 'comparative history'. A few of the comparisons are made with societies as remote from Europe as Polynesia, though only in passing and with considerable caution (*'ne transportons pas les Antipodes tout entiers à Paris ou à Londres'*).[36] Central to the book is the comparison between France and England, the only countries in Europe where the royal touch was exercised. A comparison, it should be added, that leaves room for contrasts.

In short, Bloch was already practising in 1924 what he was to preach four years later, in an article called 'Towards a Comparative History of European Societies'. The article argues the case for what the author called 'an improved and more general use' of the comparative method, distinguishing the study of the similarities between societies from that of their differences, and the study of societies that are neighbours in space and time from that of societies that are remote from one another, but recommending historians to practise all these approaches.[37]

Febvre on Renaissance and Reformation   After completing his old project on historical geography, Febvre, like Bloch, shifted his interests to the study of collective attitudes, or 'historical psychology', as he (like his friend Henri Berr) sometimes called it.[38] For the rest of his life he would concentrate his serious research on the history of the Renaissance and the Reformation, particularly in France.

He began this phase in his career with four lectures on the early French Renaissance, a biography of Luther, and a polemical article on the origins of the French Reformation, which he described as 'a badly-put question' (une question mal posée). All these contributions focused on social history and collective psychology.

The lectures on the Renaissance, for example, rejected the traditional explanations of this movement provided by historians of literature and art (including his old master Emile Mâle), and stressing internal evolution. Instead, Febvre offered a social explanation for this 'revolution', emphasizing what might be called the 'demand' for new ideas, and also, as in the thesis on Franche-Comté, the rise of the bourgeoisie.[39]

In a similar way, Febvre's article on the Reformation criticized ecclesiastical historians for their treatment of that movement as essentially concerned with institutional 'abuses' and their reform, rather than with 'a profound revolution in religious feeling' (une révolution profonde du sentiment religieux). The reason for this revolution, according to Febvre, was, once more, the rise of the bourgeoisie, who 'needed . . . a religion which was clear, reasonable, humane and gently fraternal'.[40] The invocation of the bourgeoisie now seems a little too glib, but the attempt to link religious to social history remains inspiring.

The reader may well be surprised to find Febvre writing a historical biography at this point in his career. However, the author's preface to the study of Luther claimed that it would not be a biography, but an attempt to solve a problem, in this case 'the problem of the relationship between the individual and the group, between personal initiative and social constraint' (la nécessité sociale). He noted the existence in 1517 of potential followers of Luther, the bourgeoisie yet again, a group who were acquiring 'a new sense of social importance' and were ill at ease with clerical mediation between God and man. All the same, Febvre refused to reduce Luther's ideas to an expression of the interests of the bourgeoisie. On the contrary, he argued that these creative ideas were not always appropriate for their social setting, and that they had to be adapted to the needs and to the mentality of the bourgeoisie by Luther's followers, notably by Melanchthon.[41]

It should be obvious by this time that certain central themes echo and re-echo in Febvre's work, and also that there was a creative tension between his fascination with individuals and his concern with groups, as there was between his strong interest in writing a social history of religion and his equally strong desire not to reduce spiritual attitudes and values to mere expressions of changes in the economy or in society.

III   THE FOUNDATION OF *ANNALES*

Shortly after the end of the First World War, Febvre had planned an international review to be devoted to economic history and to be headed by the great Belgian historian, Henri Pirenne. The project encountered difficulties and it was put aside. In 1928, it was Bloch who took the initiative in reviving the plans for a journal (a French journal this time), and on this occasion the project was successful.[42] Pirenne was again asked to direct the review but refused, so Febvre and Bloch became joint editors.

Annales d'histoire économique et sociale, as it was originally called, on the model of Vidal de la Blache's *Annales de géographie*, was planned from the first to be more than just another historical journal. It made a bid for intellectual leadership in the fields of economic and social history.[43] It was the mouth-piece, or better, the loud-speaker broadcasting the editors' pleas for a new, interdisciplinary approach to history.

The first issue was dated 15 January 1929. This issue carries a message from the editors, explaining that they had planned the journal long ago, regretting the barriers between historians and workers in other disciplines, and emphasizing the need for intellectual exchange.[44] The editorial committee included not only historians, ancient and modern, but a geographer (Albert Demangeon), a sociologist (Maurice Halbwachs), an economist (Charles Rist), and a political scientist (André Siegfried, a former pupil of Vidal de la Blache).[45]

Economic historians were prominent in the early issues – Pirenne, for example, who wrote a piece on the education of medieval merchants; the Swedish historian Eli Heckscher, author of a famous study of mercantilism; and the American Earl Hamilton, best known for his work on American treasure and the price revolution in Spain. At this point the journal looked more or less like a French equivalent, or rival, of the British *Economic History Review*. However, an announcement in 1930 declared the intention of the journal to establish itself 'on the almost virgin soil of social history' (*sur le terrain si mal défriché de l'histoire sociale*).[46] It also concerned itself with method in the social sciences, like the *Revue de Synthèse Historique*.

The emphasis on economic history suggests that Bloch was the dominant co-editor in the early years. However, without seeing the whole of their correspondence, much of it unpublished, it would be foolhardy to try to guess whether Febvre or Bloch was more important in the creation of '*Annales* history' after 1929, or even how they divided between them the labour of running the journal. What can be said with confidence is that if the two men had not agreed on fundamentals and worked well together, the movement would not have been a success. All the same, the historical contributions of the two partners after 1929 need to be considered separately.

Bloch on Rural History and Feudalism   Bloch's career was the shorter, brutally interrupted by the war. In his last decades of academic life he produced some seminal articles and two important books. The articles include a study of the water-mill, and the cultural and social obstacles to its diffusion; and reflections on technological change 'as a problem of collective psychology'.[47] Since Bloch is often seen as an economic historian, it may be worth drawing attention to his interest in psychology, most obvious in *The Royal Touch*, but also prominent in the lecture on technological change, a lecture that was delivered to a group of professional psychologists and called for collaboration between the two disciplines.[48]

Bloch's main effort went into two major books. In the first place, there was his study of French rural history. This book began as a series of lectures in Oslo at the invitation of the Institute for the Comparative Study of Civilizations there.[49] However, it was in a sense an extension in space and time of the thesis on the rural population of the Ile-de-France in the Middle Ages, which he had planned before the First World War and laid aside when he joined the army. The book, published in 1931, is little more than 200 pages long, a brief essay on a large subject, though enough to reveal the author's gift for synthesis and for getting to the essentials of a problem.

This essay was and remains important for a number of reasons. Like *The Royal Touch*, it was concerned with developments over the long term, from the thirteenth century to the eighteenth, and it made illuminating comparisons and contrasts between France and England. Bloch's conception of 'rural history' (*histoire agraire*), defined as 'the combined study of rural techniques and rural customs', was an unusually broad one for its time, when historians were more likely to write on narrower themes such as the history of agriculture, or serfdom, or landed property. Equally unusual was Bloch's systematic use of non-literary sources, such as estate maps, and his broad conception of 'rural culture' (*civilisation agraire*), a term he chose to stress the fact that the existence of different agrarian systems could not be explained in terms of the physical environment alone.[50]

French Rural History is perhaps most famous for its so-called 'regressive method'. Bloch stressed the need to 'read history backwards' (*lire l'histoire à rebours*) on the grounds that we know more about the later periods and that it is only prudent to proceed from the known to the unknown.[51] Bloch deploys this method to good effect, but he did not claim to have invented it. Under the name of the 'retrogressive method', it had already been employed by F. W. Maitland – a scholar for whom Bloch professed considerable admiration – in his classic study *Domesday Book and Beyond* (1897); the 'beyond' in the title refers to the period before the making of Domesday Book in 1086.[52]

A few years before Maitland, another study of medieval England and one still closer to Bloch's interests, Frederick Seebohm's *The English Village Community* (1883), began with a chapter on 'The English Open Field System Examined in its Modern Remains', especially in Hitchin, where Seebohm lived, before working its way back to the Middle Ages. Indeed, the ancient historian Fustel de Coulanges, the teacher of Bloch's father Gustave, had employed a similar approach in *The Ancient City* (1864), when studying the history of the Greek and Roman *gens* or lineage. He admits that all the evidence about this social group 'dates from a time when it was no longer anything but a shadow of itself', but argues that this late evidence still allows us 'to catch a glimpse' of the system in its prime.[53] In other words, Bloch did not invent a new method. What he did was to employ it in a more self-conscious and systematic manner than his predecessors.

The second study, *Feudal Society* (1939–40), is the book for which Bloch is most widely known today. It is an ambitious synthesis, dealing with some four centuries of European history, from 900 to 1300, and with a wide range of topics, many of which he had discussed elsewhere; servitude and liberty, sacred kingship, the importance of money, and so on. In this sense the book sums up his life's work. Unlike earlier studies of the feudal system, it is not confined to the relation between land tenure, the social hierarchy, warfare and the state. It deals with feudal society as a whole: with what we might now call 'the culture of feudalism'.

It also deals, once more, with historical psychology, with what the author called 'modes of feeling and thought' (*façons de sentir et de penser*). This is the most original part of the book, a discussion that deals among other topics with the medieval sense of time, or rather, medieval 'indifference to time', or at any rate the lack of interest in accurate measurement. Bloch also devotes a chapter to 'collective memory', a topic that had long fascinated him as it had fascinated his friend, the Durkheimian sociologist Maurice Halbwachs (above, p. 22).

Feudal Society is indeed Bloch's most Durkheimian book. He continues to use the language of *conscience collective, mémoire collective, représentations collectives*.[54] Incidental observations such as the following echo the master: 'in every literature, a society contemplates its own image'.[55] The book is essentially concerned with one of the central themes of Durkheim's work, social cohesion. This particular form of cohesion or of 'ties of dependence' (*liens de dépendance*) is explained in what is essentially a functionalist manner as an adaptation to the 'needs' of a particular social milieu, more precisely as a response to three waves of invasion – those of the Vikings, the Muslims and the Magyars.

Durkheim's concern with comparison, with typology and with social evolution left its mark on a section at the end of the book, entitled 'feudalism as a typical form of social organization' (*la féodalité comme type social*), in which Bloch argues that feudalism was not a unique event, but rather a recurrent phase of social evolution. With his usual caution he noted the need for more systematic analysis, but he went on to cite Japan as an example of a society which spontaneously produced a system essentially similar to that of the medieval West. He pointed out significant differences between the two societies, notably the European vassal's right to defy his lord. All the same, this concern for recurrent trends and for comparisons with remote societies makes Bloch's work very much more sociological than that of other French historians of his generation. It was indeed too sociological for Lucien Febvre, who chided Bloch for failing to discuss individuals in more detail.

IV   THE INSTITUTIONALIZATION OF *ANNALES*

In the 1930s the Strasbourg group was dispersed. Febvre left Strasbourg in 1933 to go to a chair at the prestigious Collège de France, while Bloch left in 1936 to succeed Hauser in the chair of economic history at the Sorbonne. Given the importance of Paris in French intellectual life, these moves to the centre were signs of the success of the *Annales* movement.

So was Febvre's appointment as president of the committee organizing the *Encyclopédie française*, an ambitious interdisciplinary venture which began publication in 1935. One of the most remarkable volumes of this encyclopaedia was the one edited by Febvre's old teacher, Antoine Meillet, and dealing with what might be called 'conceptual apparatus' or 'mental equipment' – in the original French, *outillage mental*. It might be said that this volume laid the base for the rise of the history of mentalities. It should be added, however, that at much the same time, Febvre's former colleague at Strasbourg, Georges Lefebvre, published an article – which was to become famous – on the study of revolutionary crowds and their collective mentalities. Irritated by the dismissal of the irrationality of crowds by the conservative psychologist Gustave Lebon, Lefebvre tried to establish the logic of their actions.

Annales gradually became the focus of a historical school. It was in the 1930s and 1940s that Febvre wrote most of his attacks on narrow empiricists and specialists, and his manifestos and programmes for the 'new kind of history' associated with *Annales* – pleading for collaborative research, for problem-oriented history (*l'histoire-problème*), for the history of sensibility, and so on.[56]

Febvre was always inclined to divide the world into those who were with him and those who were against him, and history into 'their' kind and 'ours'.[57] However, he was surely right to recognize the existence by 1939 of a group of supporters, 'a faithful nucleus of young men', who followed what they call 'the spirit of *Annales*' (*l'esprit des Annales*).[58] He was probably thinking in the first instance of Fernand Braudel, whom he had come to know in 1937, but there were others too. Pierre Goubert studied with Marc Bloch at this time, and although he came to specialize on the seventeenth century he remained faithful to Bloch's style of rural history. Some of the pupils of Bloch and Febvre at Strasbourg were now passing on their message in schools and universities. In Lyons, Maurice Agulhon studied history with one pupil of Bloch's, and Georges Duby with another. Duby has described Bloch, whom he never met, as his 'master'.[59]

These developments were halted for a time by the Second World War. Bloch's reaction, although he was fifty-three in 1939, was to rejoin the army. After the defeat of France he returned briefly to academic life, but then joined the Resistance, in which he played an active part until his capture by the Germans. He was shot in 1944. Despite his 'extramural activities', Bloch found the time to write two short books in the war years. The first, *Strange Defeat*, was an eyewitness account of the French collapse in 1940, and also an attempt to understand it from the point of view of a historian.

Even more remarkable, perhaps, was Bloch's ability to compose his calm reflections on the purpose and method of history at a time when he was increasingly isolated and anxious about the future prospects of his family, his friends and his country. This essay on 'the historian's craft' (*métier d'historien*), left unfinished at the author's death, is a lucid, moderate, and judicious introduction to the subject – still one of the best we have – rather than the manifesto for the new history Febvre would surely have written in his place.[60] The only iconoclastic feature was a section attacking what Bloch called, in the style of Simiand, 'the idol of origins', and arguing that every historical phenomenon has to be explained in terms of its own time, not an earlier one.[61]

Febvre's Rabelais   Meanwhile, Febvre was editing the journal, first in their joint names and later in his own.[62] Too old to fight, he sat out most of the war in his country cottage, writing a series of books and articles about the French Renaissance and Reformation. Several of these studies deal with individuals, such as Marguerite de Navarre and François Rabelais, but they are not biographies in the strict sense. Faithful to his precepts, Febvre organized his studies around problems. How, for example, could Marguerite, a learned and pious princess, write a collection of stories, *The Heptameron*, some of which are extremely bawdy? Was Rabelais an unbeliever or was he not?

The Problem of Unbelief in the Sixteenth Century: The Religion of Rabelais – to give the study its full title – is one of the most seminal works of history published this century. Together with Bloch's *Royal Touch* and Lefebvre's article on crowds, it inspired the history of collective mentalities with which so many French historians were to become concerned from the 1960s onwards. Like so many of Febvre's studies, it began with his reaction against the views of another historian. Febvre was irritated into concerning himself with Rabelais by coming across the suggestion, in Abel Lefranc's edition of *Pantagruel*, that Rabelais was an unbeliever who wrote in order to undermine Christianity. Febvre was convinced that this interpretation was not only mistaken so far as Rabelais was concerned, but anachronistic as well, attributing thoughts to the author of *Pantagruel* which were not thinkable in the sixteenth century; thus he set out to refute it.

The Problem of Unbelief has a rather unusual structure, a kind of inverted pyramid. It begins in an extremely precise, philological way. According to Lefranc, the atheism of Rabelais was denounced by a number of his contemporaries, so Febvre examined these contemporaries, for the most part minor neo-Latin poets of the 1530s, to show that the term 'atheist' did not have its modern, precise meaning. It was a smear-word, 'used in whatever sense one wanted to give it'.

Widening out from this discussion of a single word, Febvre discussed the apparently blasphemous jokes that Rabelais made in *Pantagruel* and *Gargantua*, jokes that Lefranc had stressed in his argument for the author's 'rationalism'. Febvre pointed out that these jokes belonged to a medieval tradition of the parody of the sacred in which medieval clerics had often indulged; they were not evidence of rationalism. According to Febvre, Rabelais was a Christian of an Erasmian kind: a critic of many of the outward forms of the late medieval Church, but a believer in interior religion.

At this point one might have expected the book to come to an end, since the religious credentials of Rabelais had been verified and Lefranc's arguments refuted. What Febvre actually did was to widen his investigation still further. Leaving Rabelais behind, he went on to discuss what he called the impossibility of atheism in the sixteenth century. Marc Bloch had attempted to explain why people continued to believe in the miracle of the royal touch – even when cures failed to take place. In similar fashion, Febvre now tried to explain why people did not doubt the existence of God. He argued that the *outillage mental* of the period, its 'conceptual apparatus', as he called it, did not allow unbelief. Febvre approached the problem, with characteristic verve, by a sort of *via negativa*, noting the importance of what was lacking in the sixteenth century, the 'missing words' (*mots qui manquent*), including such key terms as 'absolute' and 'relative', 'abstract' and 'concrete', 'causality', 'regularity', and many more. 'Without them', he asks rhetorically, 'how could anyone's thought be given a truly philosophical vigour, solidity and clarity?'

Febvre's lifelong interest in linguistics underlies this extremely original discussion. However, he was not content with a linguistic analysis. The book ended with a discussion of some problems of historical psychology. It is this part of the book that is best known, most controversial, and most inspiring. Febvre observed, for example, that sixteenth-century conceptions of space and time were by our standards extremely imprecise. 'What year was Rabelais born? He did not know', and there was nothing unusual in that. 'Measured time', or clock time, was still less significant than 'experienced time', described in terms of sunrise, the flight of the woodcocks, or the length of an Ave Maria. Febvre went still further, and suggested that sight was an 'undeveloped' sense in this period, and that a sense of the beauty of nature was lacking. 'There was no Hotel Bellevue in the sixteenth century, nor any Hotel Beau Site. They were not to appear until the age of Romanticism.'

According to Febvre, there was a still more significant absence from the world-view of the period. 'No one then had a sense of what was impossible' – I take it that Febvre is arguing that there were no generally accepted criteria for what was impossible, for the adjective 'impossible' was not one of his 'missing words'. As a result of this lack of criteria, what we call 'science' was literally unthinkable in the sixteenth century. 'Let us guard against projecting this modern conception of science onto the learning of our ancestors.' The conceptual apparatus of the period was too 'primitive'. Thus a precise and technical analysis of the meaning of the term 'atheist' in a handful of writers has led to a bold characterization of the world-view of an entire age.

After nearly fifty years, Febvre's book now seems somewhat dated. Later historians have noted evidence that he missed, suggesting that Rabelais had considerable sympathy for some of Luther's ideas. Others have questioned Febvre's assumption of the unthinkability of atheism in the sixteenth century, drawing on interrogations by the Inquisition in Spain and Italy and pointing to individuals who seem at least to have denied Providence or to have professed a form of materialism.[63] The theory of the underdevelopment of the visual – taken up twenty years later by the Canadian media theorist Marshall McLuhan – is not very plausible. Whether or not there was a Hotel Bellevue in sixteenth-century France, there was certainly a Belvedere in Renaissance Florence, while Alberti and others argued that the eye was pre-eminent over the ear.

Most serious of all is the criticism that Febvre assumed rather too easily a homogeneity of thought and feeling among the twenty million French people of the period, writing confidently about 'the men of the sixteenth century' (*les hommes du XVIe siècle*) as if there were no significant differences between the assumptions of men and women, rich and poor, and so on.[64]

Yet Febvre's book remains exemplary, for the questions it asks and the methods by which it pursues them rather than for the answers it gives. It is an outstanding example of problem-oriented history. Like Bloch's *Royal Touch*, it has exercised considerable influence on historical writing in France and elsewhere. Ironically enough, it does not seem to have had much effect on Fernand Braudel, to whom the book was dedicated, 'in hope'. However, the history of mentalities, as practised from the 1960s onwards by Georges Duby, Robert Mandrou, Jacques Le Goff and many others, owes a good deal to the example of Febvre as well as to that of Bloch.

Febvre in Power   After the war, Febvre was given his opportunity at last. He was invited to help reorganize one of the leading institutions in the French system of higher education, the Ecole Pratique des Hautes Etudes, founded in 1884. He was elected a member of the Institute. He also became French delegate at UNESCO, involved with the organization of a multi-volume 'Scientific and Cultural History of Mankind'. Given all these activities, Febvre had little time to write at length and the projects of his later years never came to fruition (like the volume on 'Western Thought and Belief' from 1400 to 1800), or were finished by others. The history of the printed book and its effects on Western culture in the age of the Renaissance and Reformation was largely the work of Febvre's collaborator, Henri-Jean Martin, although published under their joint names.[65] The essay on historical psychology, *Introduction to Modern France*, was written on the basis of Febvre's notes by his pupil Robert Mandrou, and published under the latter's name.[66]

However, Febvre's greatest achievement in the post-war years was to set up the organization within which 'his' kind of history could develop, the Sixth Section, founded in 1947, of the Ecole Pratique des Hautes Etudes. Febvre became president of the Sixth Section, concerned with the social sciences, and director of the Centre des Recherches Historiques, which was a section within the section. He placed his disciples and friends in key positions in the organization. Braudel, whom he treated as a son, helped him administer the Centre des Recherches Historiques as well as *Annales*. Charles Morazé, a historian of the nineteenth century, joined him in the small 'Directing Committee' of the journal. Robert Mandrou, another of Febvre's 'sons', became its organizing secretary in 1955, just before Febvre's death.

Annales had begun as the journal of a heretical sect. 'It is necessary to be a heretic', Febvre declared in his inaugural lecture, *Oportet haereses esse*.[67] After the war, however, the journal turned into the official organ of an orthodox Church.[68] Under Febvre's leadership the intellectual revolutionaries were able to take over the French historical Establishment. The inheritor of his power would be Fernand Braudel.

3

The Age of Braudel

I *THE MEDITERRANEAN*

In 1929, when *Annales* was founded, Fernand Braudel was twenty-seven years old. He had studied history at the Sorbonne, he was teaching in a school in Algeria, and he was working on his thesis. This thesis had begun as a fairly conventional – if ambitious – piece of diplomatic history. It was originally planned as a study of Philip II and the Mediterranean; in other words, an analysis of the king's foreign policy.

During its long period of gestation, the thesis became much broader in scope. It was and is normal for French academic historians to teach in schools while they write up their theses. Lucien Febvre, for example, taught briefly in Besançon. Braudel spent the ten years 1923–32 teaching in Algeria, and the experience seems to have widened his horizons.

At all events, his first important article, published in this period, dealt with the Spaniards in North Africa in the sixteenth century. This study, which is actually the size of a small book, deserves to be rescued from an undeserved neglect. It was at once a critique of his predecessors in the field for their over-emphasis on battles and great men, a discussion of the 'daily life' of the Spanish garrisons, and a demonstration of the close (if inverse) relation between African and European history. When war broke out in Europe, the African campaigns were halted, and vice versa.[1]

Much of the fundamental research for the thesis was done in the early 1930s in Simancas, where the Spanish state papers are kept, and in the archives of the leading cities of the Christian Mediterranean – Genoa, Florence, Palermo, Venice, Marseilles, and Dubrovnik, where Braudel saved time by filming the documents (when permitted) with an American cine-camera.[2]

This research was interrupted by a spell teaching at the University of São Paulo (1935–7), which Braudel later described as the happiest time of his life. It was on the voyage back from Brazil that Braudel made the acquaintance of Lucien Febvre, who adopted him as an intellectual son (*un enfant de la maison*) and persuaded him, if he still needed persuading, that 'Philip II and the Mediterranean' should really be 'The Mediterranean and Philip II'.[3]

The Making of *The Mediterranean* It was, ironically enough, the Second World War that gave Braudel the opportunity to write his thesis. He spent most of the war years in a prisoner-of-war camp near Lübeck. His prodigious memory compensated to some extent for his lack of access to libraries, and he drafted *The Mediterranean* in longhand in exercise books which he posted to Febvre, to reclaim after the war.[4] Only a historian who has examined the manuscripts can say what relation they bear to the thesis that Braudel defended in 1947 and published in 1949 (dedicated to Febvre 'with the affection of a son'). My concern here is with the printed text.

The Mediterranean is a massive book, even by the standards of the traditional French doctoral thesis. In its original edition, it already contained some 600,000 words, making it six times the length of an ordinary book. It is divided into three parts, each of which – as the preface points out – exemplifies a different approach to the past. In the first place, there is the 'almost timeless' history of the relationship between 'man' and the 'environment', then the gradually changing history of economic, social and political structures, and finally the fast-moving history of events. It may be useful to discuss these three parts in reverse order.

The third part, which is the most traditional, probably corresponds to Braudel's original idea of a thesis on Philip II's foreign policy. Braudel offers his readers a highly professional piece of political and military history. He provides brief but incisive character-sketches of the leading characters on the historical stage, from the 'narrow-minded and politically short-sighted' Duke of Alba, *'ce faux grand homme'*, to his master, Philip II, slow, 'solitary and secretive', cautious, hard-working, a man who 'saw his task as an unending succession of small details', but lacked a vision of the larger whole. The battle of Lepanto, the siege and relief of Malta, and the peace negotiations of the late 1570s are all described at considerable length.

However, this narrative of events is further removed from traditional 'drum and trumpet' history than it may appear at first sight. Time after time, the author goes out of his way to emphasize the insignificance of events and the limitations on the freedom of action of individuals. In 1565, for example, Don García de Toledo, the Spanish naval commander in the Mediterranean, was slow to relieve Malta from its siege by the Turks. 'Historians have blamed Don García for his delay', writes Braudel, 'but have they always examined thoroughly the conditions under which he had to operate?'[5] Again, he insists that Philip II's well-known and oft-condemned slowness to react to events is not to be explained entirely in terms of his temperament, but has to be viewed in relation to Spain's financial exhaustion, and to the problems of communication over such a vast empire.[6]

In similar fashion, Braudel refuses to explain in personal terms the success of Don Juan – Don John of Austria – at Lepanto. Don Juan was merely 'the instrument of destiny' in the sense that his victory depended on factors of which he was not even aware.[7] In any case, according to Braudel, Lepanto was only a naval victory, which 'could not destroy Turkey's roots, which went deep into the continental interior'.[8] It was only an event. Again, Don Juan's capture of Tunis is described as 'another victory which led nowhere'.

Braudel is concerned to place individuals and events in context, in their milieu, but he makes them intelligible at the price of revealing their fundamental unimportance. The history of events, he suggests, although 'the richest in human interest', is also the most superficial. 'I remember a night near Bahia when I was enveloped in a firework display of phosphorescent fireflies; their pale lights glowed, went out, shone again, all without piercing the night with any true illumination. So it is with events; beyond their glow, darkness prevails.'[9] In another poetic image, Braudel described events as 'surface disturbances, crests of foam that the tides of history carry on their strong backs'. 'We must learn to distrust them.'[10] To understand the past it is necessary to dive beneath the waves.

The stiller waters that run deeper are the subject of the second part of *The Mediterranean*, entitled 'Collective Destinies and General Trend's (*Destins collectifs et mouvements d'ensemble*), and concerned with the history of structures – economic systems, states, societies, civilizations and the changing forms of war. This history moves at a slower pace than that of events. It moves in generations or even centuries, so that contemporaries are scarcely aware of it. All the same, they are carried along with the current. In one of his most famous pieces of analysis, Braudel examines Philip II's empire as a 'colossal enterprise of land and sea transport' which was 'exhausted by its own size', necessarily so in an age when 'the Mediterranean crossing from North to South could be expected to take one or two weeks', while the crossing from East to West took 'two or three months'.[11] One is reminded of Gibbon's verdict on the Roman Empire as crushed by its own weight, and of his remarks on geography and communications in the first chapter of the *Decline and Fall*.

Yet the sixteenth century seems to have been an environment that favoured large states, states like the opposing Spanish and Turkish empires which dominated the Mediterranean. 'The course of history', according to Braudel, 'is by turns favourable and unfavourable to vast political hegemonies', and the period of economic growth during the fifteenth and sixteenth centuries created a situation consistently favourable to the large and very large state.[12]

Like their political structures, the social structures of the two great empires – opposed to each other in so many ways – came to resemble each other more and more. The main social trends in

Anatolia and the Balkans in the sixteenth and seventeenth centuries parallel the trends in Spain and Italy (much of which was under Spanish rule at this time). The basic trend in both areas, according to Braudel, was one of economic and social polarization. The nobility prospered and migrated to the towns, while the poor grew poorer and were increasingly driven to piracy and banditry. As for the middle class, they disappeared or 'defected' to the nobility, a process described by Braudel as the 'treason' or the 'bankruptcy' of the bourgeoisie (*trahison, faillite de la bourgeoisie*).[13]

Braudel extends this comparison between the Christian and Muslim Mediterraneans from society to 'civilization', as he calls it, in a chapter that concentrates on cultural frontiers and the gradual diffusion of ideas, objects, or customs across these barriers. Avoiding any facile diffusionism, he also discusses the resistance to these innovations, with special reference to the Spanish 'refusal' of Protestantism, the rejection of Christianity on the part of the Moors of Granada, and the Jews' resistance to all other civilizations.[14]

We have still not reached the bottom. Beneath the social trends there lies yet another history, 'a history whose passage is almost imperceptible . . . a history in which all change is slow, a history of constant repetition, ever-recurring cycles'.[15] The true bedrock of the study is this history 'of man in his relationship to the environment', a kind of historical geography, or, as Braudel prefers to call it, 'geo-history'. Geo-history is the subject of Part One of *The Mediterranean*, which devotes some 300 pages to mountains and plains, coastlines and islands, climate, land-routes, and sea-routes.

This part of the book doubtless owes its existence to Braudel's love affair with the region, revealed in his very first sentence, beginning 'I have loved the Mediterranean with passion, no doubt because I am a northerner' (Braudel came from Lorraine). All the same, it has its place in the plan. The aim is to show that all these geographical features have their history, or rather, that they are part of history, and that neither the history of events nor the general trends can be understood without them. The section on mountains, for example, discusses the culture and society of the mountain regions; the cultural conservatism of the mountaineers, the social and cultural barriers between mountaineers and plainsmen, and the need for many of the young highlanders to emigrate and to become mercenary soldiers.[16]

Turning to the sea itself, Braudel contrasts the western Mediterranean, which was under Spanish domination in this period, with the eastern Mediterranean, which was subject to the Turk. 'Politics merely followed the outline of an underlying reality. These two Mediterraneans, commanded by warring rulers, were physically, economically and culturally different from each other.'[17] Yet the Mediterranean region remains a unity, more of a unity (according to Braudel) than Europe, thanks to the climate and to the wines and olives which flourish in it, as well as to the sea itself.

This remarkable volume caused an immediate sensation in the French historical world. Its reputation has spread in increasing ripples to other disciplines and other parts of the globe (below, pp. 94). There can be no doubt of its originality. All the same, as the author acknowledged in his bibliographical essay, his book does have a place in a tradition, or more exactly in several different traditions.

In the first place, of course, the tradition of *Annales*, a journal that was twenty years old when the book was published. 'What I owe to the *Annales*, to their teaching and inspiration, constitutes the greatest of my debts.'[18] The first part of the book, on the role of the environment, is heavily indebted to the French geographical school, from Vidal de la Blache himself, whose pages on the Mediterranean Braudel 'read and reread', to the regional monographs inspired by the master.[19] Lucien Febvre is also present in this part of *The Mediterranean*, not only as the author of an essay on historical geography, but because his thesis on Philip II and Franche-Comté had begun with a geographical introduction of a similar kind, though on a far smaller scale.

An equally palpable presence in *The Mediterranean*, ironically enough, is the man Febvre loved to attack, the German geographer Friedrich Ratzel, whose ideas on geo-politics seem to have helped Braudel formulate his ideas on a number of themes, from empires to islands.[20] Sociologists and anthropologists are less visible, but the chapter on Mediterranean civilization shows signs of the author's debt to the ideas of Marcel Mauss.[21]

Among historians, Braudel probably owes most to the great Belgian medievalist Henri Pirenne, whose famous *Muhammad and Charlemagne* argued that the rise of Charlemagne, the end of the classical tradition and the making of the Middle Ages, could not be understood without going outside the history of Europe, or Christendom, and studying the Muslim Middle East. Pirenne's vision of two hostile empires confronting one another across the Mediterranean, some 800 years before Suleiman the Magnificent and Philip II, must also have been an inspiration for Braudel. Curiously enough, although this was Pirenne's last book, the idea for it came to him in a prison camp during the First World War, while Braudel worked on his in a prison camp in the Second World War.[22]

Evaluations of *The Mediterranean*   Braudel complained in his second edition that he had been much praised and little criticized. There have been criticisms, however, some of them cogent, from the United States and elsewhere.[23] At the level of detail, a number of Braudel's arguments have been challenged by later researchers. The thesis about the 'bankruptcy of the bourgeoisie', for example, does not satisfy historians of the Low Countries, where merchants continued to flourish. Again, Braudel's thesis about the relative insignificance of the battle of Lepanto has been qualified, if not exactly rejected, by recent work.[24]

Another lacuna in *The Mediterranean* has attracted less attention, but it requires emphasis here. Despite his aspirations towards what he liked to call a 'total history', Braudel has remarkably little to say about attitudes, values, or *mentalités collectives*, even in the chapter devoted to 'Civilizations'. In this respect he differs greatly from Febvre, despite his praise for *The Problem of Unbelief*.[25]

For example, Braudel has virtually no comment to make about honour, shame and masculinity, although (as a number of anthropologists have shown) this system of values was (and indeed still is) of great importance in the Mediterranean world, Christian and Muslim alike.[26] Although religious beliefs, Catholic and Muslim, obviously mattered in the Mediterranean world in the age of Philip II, Braudel does not discuss them at any length. Despite his interest in cultural frontiers, he has curiously little to say about the relation between Christianity and Islam in his period. This lack of concern contrasts with the interest in the interpenetration of Christianity and Islam shown by some earlier historians of Spain and Eastern Europe, who pointed out the existence of Muslim shrines which were frequented by Christians, or of Muslim mothers who baptized their children as a safeguard against leprosy or werewolves.[27]

Other criticisms of *The Mediterranean* are still more radical. An American reviewer complained that Braudel had 'mistaken a poetic response to the past for an historical problem', so that his book lacked focus, and that the organization of the book cut events off from the geographical and social factors that explain them.[28] These criticisms are worth discussing in more detail.

The suggestion that the book fails to concern itself with a problem would be ironic indeed if well founded, since Febvre and Bloch had laid such emphasis on problem-oriented history and Braudel himself wrote elsewhere that 'The region is not the framework of research. The framework of research is the problem.'[29] Could he really have neglected his own advice? I put the question to Braudel in an interview with him in 1977, and there was no hesitation in his answer. 'My great problem, the only problem I had to resolve, was to show that time moves at different speeds.'[30] However, large parts of this massive study are not concerned with this problem, at least not directly.

The criticism of the book's three-part organization was anticipated – but not answered – by Braudel in his preface. 'If I am criticized for the method in which the book has been assembled, I hope the component parts will be found workmanlike.' A way of meeting the criticism might have been to begin with the history of events (as I have just done in my summary of the book), and show that it is unintelligible without the history of structures, which is in turn unintelligible without the history of the environment. However, to begin with what he regarded as the 'superficial' history of events would have been intolerable for Braudel. In the circumstances in which he drafted his study, in captivity, it was psychologically necessary for him to look beyond the short term.[31]

Another radical criticism of *The Mediterranean* concerns Braudel's determinism, the exact opposite of the voluntarism of Lucien Febvre. 'Braudel's Mediterranean', wrote one British reviewer, 'is a world unresponsive to human control.'[32] It is probably revealing that Braudel uses the metaphor of a prison more than once in his writings, describing man as 'prisoner' not only of his physical environment, but also of his mental framework (*les cadres mentaux aussi sont prisons de longue durée*).[33] Unlike Febvre, Braudel did not see structures as enabling as well as constraining. 'When I think of the individual', he once wrote, 'I am always inclined to see him imprisoned within a destiny [*enfermé dans un destin*] in which he himself has little hand.'[34]

It is only fair to add, however, that Braudel's determinism was not simplistic – he insisted on the need for pluralistic explanations – and also that his reviewers generally rejected this determinist view of history without offering precise or constructive criticisms. The debate over the limits of freedom and determinism is one that is likely to last as long as history is written. In this debate, whatever philosophers may say, it is extremely difficult for historians to go beyond a simple assertion of their own position.

Some critics have gone still further in their criticisms of Braudel and spoken of 'a history without humans'. To see that this accusation is exaggerated, it is only necessary to turn to the perceptive portrayals of individual character in Part Three. Yet it would surely be fair to say that the price of Braudel's Olympian view of human affairs over vast spaces and long periods is a tendency to diminish human beings, to treat them as 'human insects', a revealing phrase from the discussion of the sixteenth-century poor.[35]

A more constructive criticism of Part One of *The Mediterranean* might be to suggest that although the author admits that his geo-history is not totally immobile, he fails to show it in motion. Despite his admiration for Maximilien Sorre, a French geographer who was already concerned in the early 1940s with what he called 'human ecology', the process of interaction between humankind and the environment, Braudel fails to show us what might be called the 'making of the Mediterranean landscape', most obviously the damage done to the environment over the long term by cutting down the tree cover.[36]

It is time to turn to the more positive features of a book that even its critics generally describe as a historical masterpiece. The main point to emphasize is that Braudel has done more to change our notions of both space and time than any other historian this century.

The Mediterranean makes its readers conscious of the importance of space in history as few if any books had done before. Braudel achieved this effect by making the sea itself the hero of his epic, rather than a political unit such as the Spanish Empire, let alone an individual such as Philip II – and also by his repeated reminders of the importance of distance, of communications. Most effectively of all, Braudel helps his readers see the Mediterranean as a whole by moving outside it. The sea is vast enough in itself to drown most historians, but Braudel felt the need to extend his frontiers to the Atlantic and the Sahara. 'If we did not consider this extended zone of influence ... it would often be difficult to grasp the history of the sea.'[37] This section on the 'Greater Mediterranean', as he calls it, is a dramatic example of Braudel's conception of 'global' history, of what has been called his 'vast appetite for extending the boundaries of his undertaking', or, as he puts it himself, his 'desire and need to see on a grand scale' (*mon désir et mon besoin de voir grand*).[38] Unlike Philip II, the man obsessed with details, Braudel always had a vision of the whole.

Even more significant for historians is Braudel's original treatment of time, his attempt 'to divide historical time into geographical time, social time and individual time', and to stress the importance of what has become known (since the publication of his most famous article), as *la longue durée*.[39] Braudel's long term may be short by geologists' standards, but his emphasis on 'geographical time' in particular has opened the eyes of many historians.

The distinction between the short term and the long term had of course been common enough in the historian's vocabulary, as in ordinary language, before 1949. Indeed, studies of particular topics over several centuries were not uncommon in economic history, particularly in price history. An obvious example, well known to Braudel, is Earl J. Hamilton's *American Treasure and the Price Revolution 1501–1650* (1934). As Braudel was also aware, historians of art and literature had sometimes investigated long-term changes in culture, notably Aby Warburg and his followers in their studies of the survival and transformation of the classical tradition.[40] However, it remains Braudel's personal achievement to have combined the study of *la longue durée* with that of the complex interaction between the environment, the economy, society, politics, culture, and events.

It is the consciousness that all 'structures' are subject to change (however slow) that is, according to Braudel, the historian's special contribution to the social sciences.[41] He had little patience with frontiers, whether they separate regions or disciplines. He always wanted to see things whole, to integrate the economic, the social, the political, and the cultural into a 'total' history. 'A historian faithful to the teaching of Lucien Febvre and Marcel Mauss will always want to see the whole, the *totality* of the social.'

Few historians will want to imitate *The Mediterranean* and still fewer are capable of doing so. It is still true to say of this study, as of Tolstoy's *War and Peace* (which it resembles not only in scale but also in its awareness of space and its sense of the futility of human action), that it has permanently enlarged the possibilities of the genre in which it is written.

II   THE LATER BRAUDEL

Braudel in Power   For some thirty years, from Lucien Febvre's death in 1956 to his own death in 1985, Braudel was not only the leading French historian but also the most powerful one. He became professor at the Collège de France in 1949, the year his thesis was published, and joined Febvre as director of the Centre des Recherches Historiques at the Ecole des Hautes Etudes.[42]

From this phase of joint direction date three important series of publications by the Sixth Section (of which the Centre formed part), all of them launched in 1951–2. The first series was entitled 'Ports – Routes – Trafics', the second, 'Affaires et Gens d'Affaires', and the third, 'Monnaie – Prix – Conjoncture'. Given this strong emphasis on economic history, it is reasonable to assume that the initiative was not Febvre's, but Braudel's.[43]

After Febvre's death in 1956, Braudel succeeded him as effective director of *Annales*. The relations between Febvre's two 'sons', Braudel and Mandrou, became less and less fraternal, and Mandrou resigned from his position as organizing secretary of the journal in 1962. A major change – not to say 'purge' – was carried out in 1969, apparently in reaction to the crisis of May 1968. Events seemed to be taking their revenge on the historian who had spurned them. At all events, Braudel decided to bring in younger historians, such as Jacques Le Goff, Emmanuel le Roy Ladurie, and Marc Ferro, in order to renew *Annales*, 'faire peau neuve', as Braudel put it.[44]

Braudel also succeeded Febvre as president of the Sixth Section of the Ecole. In 1963 he founded another organization devoted to interdisciplinary research, the Maison des Sciences de l'Homme. In his day the Section, the Centre and the Maison all moved into new quarters on 54 Boulevard Raspail, where the proximity of sociologists and anthropologists of the calibre of Claude Lévi-Strauss and Pierre Bourdieu, available for conversation over coffee and for joint seminars, kept and continues to keep the *Annales* historians in touch with new developments and new ideas in neighbouring disciplines.

A man of dignified and commanding presence, Braudel remained extremely influential even after his retirement in 1972. As
for his years in office, his control over funds for research, publication and appointments gave him considerable power, which he
used to promote the ideal of a 'common market' of the social
sciences, with history as the dominant partner.[45] The scholar-
ships awarded to young historians from other countries, such
as Poland, to study in Paris helped to spread the French
style of history abroad. Braudel also made sure that historians
working on the early modern period, 1500–1800, were given at
least their fair share of resources. If his empire was not as vast as
Philip II's, it had a considerably more decisive ruler.

Braudel's influence over generations of research students must
also be taken into account. Pierre Chaunu, for example, describes
how Braudel's lectures on the history of Latin America, delivered soon after his return to France after the war, gave him such
an intellectual 'shock' that they determined his historical career.
'From the first ten minutes I was conquered, subjugated.'[46]
Chaunu is not the only historian to owe to Braudel a concern
with the early modern Mediterranean world, as well as with particular problems. For example, the author of a study of a
family of sixteenth-century Spanish merchants owed his subject
to Braudel's suggestion, while monographs on Rome and
Valladolid were inspired by his approach.[47]

Many other historians have recorded what they owed to
Braudel's advice and encouragement in the days in which they
were writing their theses. The outstanding figure in the third
generation of *Annales*, Emmanuel Le Roy Ladurie, who wrote
his thesis on the peasants of Mediterranean France, did so under
Braudel's direction. Known for a time as 'the Dauphin', Le Roy
Ladurie was to succeed Braudel at the Collège de France as
Braudel had succeeded Febvre.

The History of Material Culture   During these years of
activity as an organizer, 1949–72, Braudel was also working on
a second ambitious study. After the long years of research and
writing needed to produce the massive doctoral thesis which

used to be necessary for a successful academic career, many French historians opt for a comparatively quiet life, and produce nothing but articles or textbooks. Not so Braudel. Not long after the publication of *The Mediterranean*, Lucien Febvre had invited him to collaborate on another grand project. The idea was that the two men should write a two-volume history of Europe from 1400 to 1800, Febvre taking 'thought and belief' as his share, while Braudel would concern himself with the history of material life.[48] Febvre's part had not been written when he died in 1956; Braudel produced his in three volumes between 1967 and 1979, under the title *Civilisation matérielle et capitalisme*.[49]

Braudel's three volumes are more or less concerned with the economists' categories of consumption, distribution, and production, in that order, but he preferred to characterize them in a different way. His introduction to the first volume describes economic history as a three-storey house. On the ground floor – the metaphor is not far from Marx's 'base' – is material civilization (*civilisation matérielle*), defined as 'repeated actions, empirical processes, old methods and solutions handed down from time immemorial'. On the middle level, there is economic life (*vie économique*), 'calculated, articulated, emerging as a system of rules and almost natural necessities'. At the top – not to say 'superstructure' – there is the 'capitalist mechanism', most sophisticated of all.[50]

There are obvious parallels between the tripartite structures of *The Mediterranean* and of *Civilization and Capitalism* (as the trilogy is called). In each case the first part deals with an almost immobile history, the second part with slowly changing institutional structures, and the third part with more rapid change – with events in one book, and with trends in the other.

The first volume deals with the bottom level. Concerned as it is with an economic 'old regime' lasting some 400 years, this book, now known in English as *The Structures of Everyday Life*, exemplifies Braudel's long-standing interest in the long term.[51] It also illustrates his global approach. Originally planned as a study of Europe, the book has a little to say about Africa and a good deal about Asia and America. One of its central arguments concerns the impossibility of explaining major changes in other than global terms. Following the German economist and demographer Ernst Wagemann, Braudel noted that population movements in China and India followed a similar pattern to those of Europe: expansion in the sixteenth century, stability in the seventeenth century, and renewed expansion in the eighteenth.[52] A world-wide phenomenon obviously needs an explanation on the same scale.

While his students were studying population trends at the level of the province, or on occasion that of the village, Braudel, characteristically, was attempting to see the whole. While they were analysing subsistence crises in Europe, he was comparing the advantages and disadvantages of wheat and other grains with those of rice in the Far East and maize in America, noting, for example, that the rice-fields 'brought high populations and strict social discipline to the regions where they prospered', while maize, 'a crop that demands little effort', left the Indians 'free' (if that is the word) to labour on 'the giant Mayan or Aztec pyramids' or 'the cyclopean walls of Cuzco'.

The effect of these apparent divagations is to define Europe by contrast to the rest of the world, as a continent of grain-eaters, relatively well-equipped with furniture, a region whose density of population made transport problems less acute than elsewhere, but one where labour was relatively expensive – a stimulus to the employment of inanimate sources of energy associated with the Industrial Revolution.

In subject-matter, as in geography, Braudel bursts through the barriers of conventional economic history. He sweeps away the traditional categories of 'agriculture', 'trade' and 'industry', and looks instead at 'everyday life', at people and things, 'everything mankind makes or uses': food, clothes, housing, tools, money, towns, and so on. Two basic concepts underlie this first volume. The first is that of 'everyday life'; the second is that of 'material civilization'.

In the introduction to the second edition, Braudel declared that the aim of his book was nothing less than the historicization of everyday life (*l'introduction de la vie quotidienne dans la domaine de l'histoire*). He was not, of course, the first person to attempt this. *La civilisation quotidienne* was the title of one volume of Lucien Febvre's *Encyclopédie française*, a volume to which Bloch contributed an essay on the history of food. A series of histories of daily life in different places and times was published by Hachette from 1938 onwards, beginning with a study of the French Renaissance by Abel Lefranc (the man whose view of Rabelais so irritated Lucien Febvre). Earlier still, an important study of daily life in Denmark and Norway in the sixteenth century was made by the great Danish historian T. F. Troels-Lund, with separate volumes devoted to food, clothes, and housing.[53] All the same, Braudel's work is important for its synthesis between what might be called the 'little history' of daily life, which can easily become purely descriptive, anecdotal, or antiquarian, with the history of the great economic and social trends of the time.

Braudel's concept of *civilisation matérielle* also deserves closer analysis. The idea of a realm of routine (*Zivilisation*), as opposed to a realm of creativity (*Kultur*), was dear to Oswald Spengler, a historian with whom Braudel has more in common than is generally admitted.[54] Braudel does not concern himself with mental routines, with what Febvre called *outillage mental*. As we have seen (p. 39), Braudel has never shown great interest in the history of mentalities, and in any case he was supposed to leave thought and belief to his partner. On the other hand, he had much to say about other forms of habit.

As in his *Mediterranean*, Braudel's approach to civilization in this book is essentially that of a geographer, or geo-historian, interested in culture-areas (*aires culturelles*), between which exchanges of goods take place – or fail to take place. One of his most fascinating examples is that of the chair, which arrived in China, probably from Europe, in the second or third century AD, and was in widespread use by the thirteenth century. This acquisition required new kinds of furniture (such as high tables), and new postures – in short, a new way of life. The Japanese, on the other hand, resisted the chair, just as the Moors of Granada, discussed in *The Mediterranean*, resisted Christianity.[55]

If anything important is lacking in this brilliant study of

'material culture', as it has become customary to call it in English, it is surely the realm of symbols.[56] The American sociologist Thorstein Veblen devoted an important part of his *Theory of the Leisure Class* (1899) to a discussion of status symbols. Some historians have moved in the same direction; Lawrence Stone, for example, in a book published two years before Braudel's, discussed the houses and the funerals of the English aristocracy from this point of view.[57] More recently, historians and anthropologists alike have been devoting considerable attention to the meanings of material culture.[58]

A historical anthropologist or anthropological historian might want to supplement Braudel's fascinating account of 'carnivorous Europe', for example, with a discussion of the symbolism of such 'noble' foods as venison and pheasant, which were associated with the aristocratic pastime of hunting and played an important part in the rituals of gift exchange. Similar points might be made about the uses of clothes for what the sociologist Erving Goffman has called the 'presentation of self in everyday life', and also about the symbolism of houses, their façades and their interior arrangements.[59]

Braudel on Capitalism   *The Wheels of Commerce* opens with an evocation of the bustle and confusion of the noisy, animated, polyglot, multicoloured world of the traditional market, and continues with descriptions of fairs, pedlars and great merchants. Many of these merchants were as exotic as the goods they bought and sold, for international trade was often in the hands of outsiders – Protestants in France, Jews in Central Europe, Old Believers in Russia, Copts in Egypt, Parsees in India, Armenians in Turkey, Portuguese in Spanish America, and so on.

Here as elsewhere, Braudel kept a fine balance between the abstract and the concrete, the general and the particular. He interrupted his panorama from time to time to focus on case studies, including an agricultural 'factory', as he calls it, in the eighteenth-century Veneto, and also the Amsterdam Bourse, that 'confusion of confusions', as a seventeenth-century participant described it, already inhabited by bulls and bears. Braudel always had an eye for the vivid detail. During the fair of Medina del Campo in Castile, so he tells us, Mass used to be celebrated on the balcony of the cathedral so that 'buyers and sellers could follow the service without having to stop business'.

These colourful descriptions are complemented by a fascinating analysis in which Braudel displayed to the full his remarkable gift for appropriating ideas from other disciplines and making them his own. In *The Wheels of Commerce* he drew on the 'central-place theory' of the German geographer Walter Christaller to discuss the distribution of markets in China. He drew on the sociology of Georges Gurvitch to analyse what he calls 'the pluralism of societies', the contradictions in their social structures. He drew on the theories of Simon Kuznets, an economist 'convinced of the explanatory value of the long term in economics ... a development after my own heart', to characterize pre-industrial societies by the lack of fixed, durable capital.[60] He drew most of all from that remarkable polymath Karl Polanyi, who was studying economic anthropology in the 1940s, but argued against him that the market economy coexisted with the non-market economy in the early modern world, rather than emerging suddenly in what Polanyi called the 'great transformation' of the nineteenth century.[61]

In this account of the mechanisms of distribution and exchange, Braudel characteristically offered explanations that were at once structural and multilateral. Discussing the role of religious minorities like the Huguenots and the Parsees in international trade, he concluded that 'it is surely the social machinery itself which reserves to outsiders such unpleasant but socially essential tasks ... if they had not existed, it would have been necessary to invent them'.[62] He had no time for explanations in terms of individuals. On the other hand, Braudel remained opposed to explanations in terms of a single factor. 'Capitalism cannot have emerged from a single confined source', he remarked, sweeping away Marx and Weber with a single flick of the wrist. 'Economics played a part, politics played a part, society played a part, and culture and civilization played a part. So too did history, which often decides in the last analysis who will win a trial of strength.'[63] This is a characteristic passage of Braudel, combining open-mindedness with a lack of analytical rigour, and giving weight to factors that receive little serious discussion elsewhere in the book.

It is also a reminder that he found it necessary to preserve a certain intellectual distance from Marx and even more from Marxism, to avoid being trapped inside an intellectual framework he regarded as too rigid. 'Marx's genius, the secret of his long sway,' wrote Braudel, 'lies in the fact that he was the first to construct true social models, on the basis of a historical *longue durée*. These models have been frozen in all their simplicity by being given the status of laws.'[64]

The *Perspective of the World* shifted attention from structure to process – the process of the rise of capitalism. In this final volume, in which it was necessary to be conclusive, Braudel underplayed his usual eclectic approach. Instead, he drew heavily on the ideas of one man, Immanuel Wallerstein. Wallerstein is almost as difficult to classify as Polanyi. Trained as a sociologist, he did research in Africa. Convinced that he could not understand Africa without analysing capitalism, he turned to economics. Discovering that he could not understand capitalism without going back to its origins, he decided to become an economic historian. His unfinished history of the 'world economy' since 1500 is in its turn indebted to Braudel (to whom the second volume is dedicated).[65]

However, Wallerstein's analysis of the history of capitalism also draws on the work of development economists such as André Gunder Frank, notably on their concepts of economic 'cores' and 'peripheries' and their argument that the development of the West and the underdevelopment of the rest of the world are opposite sides of the same coin.[66] Wallerstein discusses what he calls the 'international division of labour' and the successive hegemonies of the Dutch, the British, and of the United States. He stands in a Marxist tradition, and it was something of a surprise for many readers to see the old Braudel, who had always kept his distance from Marx, finally accepting something like a Marxist framework.

The Perspective of the World is also concerned with the sequence of preponderant powers, but it begins, as one might have expected Braudel to begin, with the Mediterranean. According to him, it was fifteenth-century Venice that first achieved hegemony over a world economy. Venice was followed by Antwerp and Antwerp by Genoa, whose bankers controlled the economic destinies of Europe (and, through Spain, of America) in the late sixteenth and early seventeenth centuries, 'the age of the Genoese'. Fourth in sequence comes the Dutch Republic, or, more exactly, Amsterdam, which Braudel sees as the last of the economically dominant cities. Finally, with a characteristically skilful twist, he turns the problem inside out and discusses the failure of other parts of the world (including France and India) to achieve a similar dominant position, ending his story with Britain and the Industrial Revolution.

It is not difficult to find inaccuracies or lacunae in these volumes, particularly when the author moved away from the Mediterranean world which he knew and loved best. Such inaccuracies were virtually inevitable in a work of such breathtaking scope. A more serious criticism, analogous to the one of *The Mediterranean* offered above, is that Braudel remained, in one of his favourite metaphors, a 'prisoner' of his original division of labour with Febvre (if not of his own *outillage mental*). He continued to the end to be 'allergic', as he put it, to Max Weber, and to have little to say about capitalist values – industry, thrift, discipline, enterprise, and so on. Yet the contrast between what might be called 'pro-enterprise cultures', such as the Dutch Republic and Japan, and 'anti-enterprise cultures', such as Spain and China, is a striking one, and these differences in values are surely relevant to these countries' economic histories.

This unwillingness to allow autonomy to culture, to ideas, is clearly illustrated in one of Braudel's late essays. Discussing the problem of the rejection of the Reformation in France (as he had once discussed the rejection of the Reformation in Spain), he offered a crudely reductionist geographical explanation. He confined himself to noting that the Rhine and the Danube were the frontiers of Catholicism as they had been the frontiers of the Roman Empire, without taking the trouble to analyse the possible relation between these frontiers and the events and ideas of the Reformation.[67]

Yet the positive features of Braudel's trilogy far outweigh their defects. Together, the three volumes make a magnificent synthesis of the economic history of early modern Europe – in a wide sense of the term 'economic' – and they place this history in a comparative context. They confirmed the author's right to the world heavyweight title. One can only be grateful for this demonstration that it is still possible in the late twentieth century to resist the pressures towards specialization. One can only admire the tenacity with which Braudel carried out two large-scale projects over a period of more than fifty years.

What is more, he had not finished. In his old age, Leopold von Ranke turned to world history. For once more modest in his ambitions, Braudel embarked in his late seventies on a total history of his own nation. Only the geographical, demographic and economic sections were in existence when the author died in 1985, but they have been published under the title *The Identity of France*.

This last book was in a sense predictable – it is not difficult to imagine what a Braudelian study of France might be like. It drew, like his earlier books, on the work of his favourite geographers, from Vidal de la Blache to Maximilien Sorre. Although Braudel took the opportunity to reply to the criticism that he was an extreme determinist, and had some good words to say for 'possibilism' in the manner of Febvre and Vidal de la Blache, he did not in fact budge from his position, and reiterated his belief that we are 'crushed' by 'the enormous weight of distant origins'. All the same, the first volume of this study is another impressive demonstration of Braudel's capacity to incorporate space into history, to discuss distance and regional diversity on the one hand, communications and national cohesion on the other, and of course to offer his reflections on the changing frontiers of France over the very long term, from 843 to 1761.[68]

One last theme in Braudel's work deserves discussion here: statistics. Braudel gave a warm welcome to the quantitative methods employed by his colleagues and pupils. He made use of statistics on occasion, particularly in the second, enlarged edition of his *Mediterranean*, published in 1966. However, it would not be unfair to say that figures formed part of the decoration of his historical edifice, rather than part of its structure.[69] In a sense he resisted quantitative methods just as he resisted most forms of cultural history, dismissing Burckhardt's famous *Civilization of the Renaissance in Italy* as 'up in the air' (*aérienne, suspendue*).[70] He was thus something of a stranger to two major developments within *Annales* history in his time: quantitative history and the history of mentalities. It is time to turn to these developments.

III THE RISE OF QUANTITATIVE HISTORY

Despite his achievements and his charismatic leadership, the development of the *Annales* movement in Braudel's day cannot be explained solely in terms of his ideas, interests, and influence. The 'collective destinies and general trends' of the movement also deserve examination. Of these trends, the most important, from 1950 or thereabouts to the 1970s or even later, was surely the rise of quantitative history. This 'quantitative revolution', as it has been called, was first visible in the economic field, especially the history of prices. From the economic sphere it spread to social history, especially the history of population. Finally, in the third generation, discussed in the next chapter, the new trend penetrated cultural history – the history of religion and the history of mentalities.[71]

The Importance of Ernest Labrousse For economic historians to concern themselves with statistics was nothing new. A considerable amount of research on the history of prices had been carried out in the nineteenth century.[72] The early 1930s witnessed an explosion of interest in the subject, doubtless connected with such phenomena of the day as German hyper-inflation and the Great Crash of 1929. Two important studies of prices appeared in French in the years 1932–3. The first, which Lucien Febvre described as a book historians needed at their bedside, was called *Researches on the General Movement of Prices*.[73] It was the work of the economist François Simiand, the man who had published a resounding attack on traditional history thirty years earlier (above, p. 10). The *Researches* discussed the alternation in history of periods of expansion, which Simiand called 'A-phases', and periods of contraction, or 'B-phases'.[74]

The second important study, modestly entitled *Sketch of the Movement of Prices and Revenues in 18th-Century France*, was the work of a young historian, Ernest Labrousse.[75] Labrousse, who was two years older than Braudel, was extremely influential on historical writing in France for more than fifty years. Given his influence on younger historians of the group, many of whose theses he directed, Labrousse might be said to have been absolutely central to *Annales*. In another sense, Labrousse might be located on the margin of the group. He taught at the Sorbonne, he was concerned with the French Revolution (the event *par excellence*), and, more important still, he was a Marxist.[76]

As we have seen, neither Febvre nor Bloch took a great interest in the ideas of Karl Marx. Despite his socialism and his admiration for Jaurès, Febvre was too much of a voluntarist to find Marx illuminating. As for Bloch, despite his enthusiasm for economic history, he was separated from Marx by his Durkheimian approach.[77] Braudel, as we have seen, owed more to Marx, but only in his later work.

It was with Labrousse that Marxism began to penetrate the *Annales* group. So did statistical methods, for Labrousse was inspired by the economists Albert Aftalion and François Simiand to undertake a rigorously quantitative study of the economy of eighteenth-century France, published in two parts, the *Sketch* (1933), dealing with price movements from 1701 to 1817, and *The Crisis* (1944), dealing with the end of the old regime. These books, which are packed with tables and graphs, are concerned both with long-term trends (*le mouvement de longue durée*) and with short-term cycles, 'cyclical crises' and 'intercycles'. Labrousse, who showed great ingenuity in finding ways to measure economic trends, made use of the concepts, methods and theories of economists such as Juglar and Kondratieff, concerned respectively with short and long economic cycles, and his own teacher

Albert Aftalion, who had written on economic crises. Labrousse argued that in eighteenth-century France a bad harvest would have a 'knock-on' effect, leading to a decline in rural revenues and so a decline in the still largely rural market for industry. He also argued for the importance of the economic crisis of the late 1780s as a precondition for the French Revolution.[78] His two monographs were pioneering studies of what the *Annales* historians would later call *conjoncture* (see Glossary). They have been criticized on occasion for forcing the data to fit the model, but they have been extremely influential.

In his famous essay on 'History and the Social Sciences' (1958), which centred on the concept of *longue durée*, Braudel called Labrousse's *Crisis* 'the greatest work of history to have appeared in France in the course of the last twenty-five years'.[79] Similarly, Pierre Chaunu declared that 'The whole movement towards quantitative history in France derives from two books which were the breviaries of my generation, the *Sketch* and *The Crisis*', books that he considered more influential than *The Mediterranean* itself.[80]

These books were extremely technical, and Labrousse published relatively little thereafter. He was a historian's historian. He was not a narrow specialist, however. His interests extended well beyond the economic history of the eighteenth century, to the revolutions of 1789 and 1848 and to the social history of the European bourgeoisie from 1700 to 1850.[81] He once declared that 'there can be no study of society without a study of mentalities'.[82]

Labrousse devoted a good deal of time to the supervision of graduate students, and he deserves to be remembered as the 'grey eminence' of *Annales*, playing Father Joseph, the self-effacing but indispensable collaborator, to Braudel's Cardinal Richelieu. There are grounds for suspecting Labrousse's influence on the second edition of Braudel's *Mediterranean*, published in 1966, which placed more emphasis on quantitative history as well as including tables and graphs which the first edition lacked.[83] It was also to include more tables and graphs than before that *Annales* began to appear in enlarged format in 1969.

It is impossible to discuss in detail all the works of the 1950s and 1960s which bear the joint impress of Braudel and Labrousse, but equally impossible to leave out Chaunu's *Seville and the Atlantic* (1955–60), perhaps the longest historical thesis ever written.[84] Chaunu's study, written with the help of his wife Huguette, tried to imitate if not to surpass Braudel by taking as his region the Atlantic Ocean. He concentrated on what can be measured, the tonnage of goods transported between Spain and the New World from 1504 to 1650, widening out from this base to discuss more general fluctuations in the volume of trade, and finally the major economic trends of the period, notably the shift from expansion in the sixteenth century (an A-phase, as Simiand would say) to contraction in the seventeenth (a B-phase).

This massive study, which launched that famous pair of terms *structure* and *conjoncture*, was at once an application to transatlantic trade of a method and a model developed by Labrousse for eighteenth-century France, and a challenge to Braudel, studying an ocean, at least from an economic point of view, and taking a truly global view of his subject. The long section on the historical geography of Spanish America is also outstanding. Chaunu is second only to Braudel in his awareness of the importance of space and of communication in history.[85]

Historical Demography and Demographic History The history of population was the second great conquest of the quantitative approach, after the history of prices. The rise of demographic history took place in the 1950s, and it owes as much to contemporary awareness of a world population explosion as the price history of the 1930s owes to the Great Crash. The development of this field, in France at least, was the joint work of demographers and historians. Louis Henry, for example, who worked at the Institut National d'Etudes Demographiques (INED), turned in the 1940s from the study of population in the present to the study of the past, and developed the method of 'family reconstitution', linking the records of births, marriages, and deaths and investigating a region and a period through case studies of families in Geneva, Normandy and elsewhere.[86] The journal of the INED, *Population*, which began publication in

1946, has always carried contributions by historians.

The first volume, for example, included a seminal article by the historian Jean Meuvret. This developed the notion of 'subsistence crisis', arguing that in France in the age of Louis XIV, these crises were regular events. A rise in grain prices would soon be followed by a rise in the death rate and a drop in the birth rate. Next came a gradual recovery, and then the next crisis.[87] The ideas of this article underlie a number of later regional studies, from Goubert on the Beauvaisis onwards. Like Labrousse, Meuvret was a historian of much greater importance for the *Annales* movement in the 1940s and 1950s than his relatively meagre published work might suggest. His monument is the work of his pupils.

Historical demography was soon linked officially to social history. In 1960, the Sixth Section founded a new historical series, 'Demography and Societies', which published a number of important monographs on regional history.

The Importance of Regional and Serial History   One of the first publications in the series 'Demography and Societies' was Pierre Goubert's thesis on *Beauvais and the Beauvaisis*. Like Chaunu, Goubert divided his study into two parts, entitled 'Structure' and 'Conjoncture'. The second part is concerned with long-term and short-term fluctuations in prices, production and population over a 'long' seventeenth century running from 1600 to 1730. It is a regional illustration of Simiand's B-phase. Goubert's juxtaposition of price and population movements shows the human consequences of economic change.

The importance of the first part is that it integrates historical demography into the social history of a region. Goubert made a careful study of population trends in a number of villages in the Beauvaisis, such as Auneuil and Breteuil. He arrived at conclusions similar to Meuvret's about the persistence of an 'old demographic regime', marked by subsistence crises every thirty years or so, to the middle of the eighteenth century, and he noted how the villagers adjusted to hard times by marrying later, thus giving the wives fewer child-bearing years.

However, Goubert did more than demonstrate the relevance

to the Beauvaisis of what were becoming the orthodox inter-
pretations of economic recession and demographic crisis in the
seventeenth century. He placed considerable emphasis on what
he called 'social demography', on the fact that the chances of survival, for example, differed from one social group to another. He
called his study a contribution to 'social history', a history concerned with everyone, not just the rich and the powerful, a point
reiterated in a later work of Goubert's, *Louis XIV and Twenty
Million Frenchmen* (1966).

The most interesting parts of the book, to my mind at least,
are the chapters on urban and rural society, on the world of tex-
tile production in Beauvais, for example, or on the peasants –
rich, middling, and poor. This careful study of social differen-
tiation and social hierarchies, which Goubert later developed in
an essay on the peasantry in the seventeenth century in the whole
of France, is an invaluable corrective to any simple view of old
regime society.[88]

Rich as it is, Goubert's social analysis stops short of total
history. The problem of 'bourgeois mentality' receives a brief
discussion but, as the author admits at the start, religion and
politics are left out. In similar fashion, most of the *Annales*-style
regional monographs of the 1960s and 1970s, a remarkable collective achievement, were virtually restricted to economic and
social history, together with geographical introductions on the
Braudel model.

Goubert dedicated his thesis to Labrousse, whose role behind
the scenes is revealed by the acknowledgements prefixed to some
of the most distinguished regional studies of the second and
third generations of *Annales*, from Pierre Vilar's Catalonia to
Emmanuel Le Roy Ladurie's Languedoc and Michel Vovelle's
Provence (discussed below).[89] These studies, which are not so
much copies from a model as individual variations on a group
theme were the most impressive achievement of the *Annales*
school in the 1960s. In this respect, they resemble the regional
monographs of the French geographical school – Demangeon's
Picardy, Sion's Normandy and so on – fifty years earlier.[90] They
also mark the re-establishment of *Annales* in the provinces, in

universities such as Caen and Rennes, Lyon and Toulouse.

Generally speaking, the regional studies combined Braudelian *structures*, Labroussian *conjoncture*, and the new historical demography.

The rural society of early modern France was studied at provincial level in Burgundy, in Provence, in Languedoc, in the Ile-de-France, in Savoy, in Lorraine.[91] There was also a cluster of monographs on early modern cities, not only in France (Amiens, Lyon, Caen, Rouen, Bordeaux) but elsewhere in the Mediterranean world (Rome, Valladolid, Venice).[92] These local studies, urban and rural, have considerable family resemblances. They tend to be divided into two parts, *structures* and *conjoncture*, and to rely heavily on sources that provide fairly homogeneous data of a kind that can be arranged in long time-series such as price trends or death rates. Hence the name 'serial history' (*histoire sérielle*) often given to this approach.[93] Looking at these theses, one can see the point of Le Roy Ladurie's remark that 'the quantitative revolution has completely transformed the craft of the historian in France'.[94]

Most of these local studies were directed by Braudel or Labrousse, and most of them deal with the early modern period. There are exceptions to both rules, however. The medievalist Georges Duby wrote one of the first of these regional monographs, concentrating on property, the social structure and the aristocratic family on the area around Macon in the eleventh and twelfth centuries. Duby's work was supervised by a former colleague of Bloch's, Charles Perrin, and inspired by historical geography.[95] The nineteenth-century Limousin has also been studied in the *Annales* manner, in a volume beginning with the geography of the region, going on to describe 'economic, social and mental structures', and concluding with an analysis of political attitudes and an account of change over time.[96]

Even in the case of early modern studies, it would be misleading to present the *Annales* school or circle as if it was completely sealed off from other historians.[97] The most obvious outsider to mention is Roland Mousnier, who has been as influential a director of research on the early modern period as Braudel and Labrousse. Mousnier published his articles in the *Revue Historique*, not in *Annales*. He was professor at the Sorbonne, not the Hautes Etudes. He was *persona non grata* to Braudel. If the *Annales* circle is a club, Mousnier is certainly not a member.

All the same, his intellectual interests overlap with theirs to a considerable degree. No French historian since Bloch has taken the comparative approach to history so seriously, whether the comparisons are neighbourly or remote. Mousnier has contrasted the political development of France and England, for example, and he has studied seventeenth-century peasant revolts not only in France, but as far afield as Russia and even China. Like the *Annales* group, Mousnier has made considerable use of social theory, from Max Weber to Talcott Parsons (he has little time for Marxism).[98]

Although his political views were well to the right, Mousnier was able to collaborate on a study of the eighteenth century with Labrousse, whose heart was always on the left. They did not agree on methods of research, let alone conclusions, but the two men shared a strong interest in the analysis of the social structure of the old regime, its 'orders' and 'classes', a topic on which they organized rival conferences.[99]

Mousnier directed a considerable number of theses in social history, on topics ranging from the eighteenth-century French soldier to a computer-based quantitative analysis of changes in the social structure of a small French town over nearly three centuries.[100] In the early 1960s, he launched a programme of collective research into peasant risings of the sixteenth and seventeenth centuries, partly to refute the Marxist interpretation of French peasant revolts put forward by the Soviet historian Boris Porshnev, whose work – published in Russian in the 1940s – was translated into French by Mousnier's rivals at the Sixth Section.[101] The works of Mousnier and his pupils generally paid more attention to politics and less to economics than the regional studies supervised by Braudel and Labrousse, and they took legal criteria more seriously and economic criteria less seriously in their analyses of the social structure. However, some of these studies are scarcely distinguishable from those of the so-called *Annales* school.[102]

Le Roy Ladurie in Languedoc   There was one major exception to the heavy emphasis on economic and social structures and conjoncture, to be found in regional studies from the *Annales* circle. Emmanuel Le Roy Ladurie's doctoral thesis on *The Peasants of Languedoc* (1966) embarked, as the author put it, upon 'the adventure of a total history' over a period of more than 200 years.[103]

Le Roy Ladurie is by common consent the most brilliant of Braudel's pupils, resembling him in a number of respects – imaginative power, wide-ranging curiosity, a multidisciplinary approach, a concern with the *longue durée* and a certain ambivalence towards Marxism. Like Braudel, he is a northerner (a Norman) in love with the south. His *Peasants of Languedoc* is built on the same scale as *The Mediterranean*, beginning, as one might expect, with an account of the geography of Languedoc, a typically Mediterranean countryside of rocks and scrub, of grain, vines and olives, of holm-oaks and chestnut trees.

Le Roy Ladurie shares with Braudel an intense interest in the physical environment, an interest that has led him to produce a remarkable comparative study of the history of climate over the long term.[104] American scientists have used the evidence of tree-rings (notably those of the giant sequoias of the far west, which sometimes live for 1,500 years) to establish long-term trends in the climate. A narrow ring means a year of drought, a wide ring a year of abundant rainfall. Le Roy Ladurie had the happy idea of juxtaposing their conclusions with those obtained from another example of 'serial history', a study of variations in the date of the wine harvests in parts of Europe. An early harvest means a warm year, a late harvest a cold one. He concluded that 'the ancient vineyards of Germany, France and Switzerland echo, far-off but in harmony, the evidence of the thousand-year-old forests of Alaska and Arizona'.[105] The parallel to Braudel's comparison of population movements in Europe and Asia is obvious enough.

On the other hand, Le Roy (as it is convenient to call him) has found it necessary to keep his intellectual distance from Braudel, just as Braudel did from Marx. He abandoned the now traditional organization of regional monographs into sections on '*structures*' and '*conjoncture*'. Instead he divided his book, which runs from 1500 to 1700, into three periods, three phases of what he calls 'a great agrarian cycle', an enormous movement of ebb and flow, rise and fall.

The first is an A-phase, a period of economic expansion fuelled by a dramatic rise in the population of the region, recovering at last from the ravages of plague in the later Middle Ages. As a contemporary put it, the people of sixteenth-century Languedoc were breeding 'like mice in a barn'. Marginal land was taken back into cultivation, and the land was also exploited more intensively. The average peasant holding became smaller and smaller (because there were more children to divide the land among), and the rural wage labourers became poorer and poorer (because the growth of population created a buyers' market for labour). The group that profited from change was that of the landowners who managed their estates themselves.

Population continued to expand, at a slower rate, till 1650 or even 1680 (some time after it had stopped rising in Goubert's Beauvaisis), and landowners to profit. Indeed, Le Roy calls the period 1600–50 that of the 'rent offensive'. At this point, however, what Simiand would call a 'B-phase' of depression occurred and the whole enormous movement went into reverse. The fundamental reason for this reversal was the decline in the productivity of agriculture. The impoverished cultivators were unable to invest in their land, and in any case there was a limit to what could be squeezed out of this rocky Mediterranean soil. There was not enough food to go round, and so there was a subsistence crisis. Many people died, some emigrated, and (as in the Beauvaisis) couples tended to marry later than before. 'It looks very much as if population was adjusting painfully to the conditions of a contracting economy.'[106] On the other hand, the decline in population intensified the economic depression, which reached its bottom in the early eighteenth century, at the close of the reign of Louis XIV. He concluded that 'The Malthusian curse had fallen on Languedoc in the sixteenth and seventeenth centuries', in the sense that the growth of population wiped out every increase in prosperity, just as Malthus said it would.[107]

What I have described above is a distinguished piece of geographical, economic and social history in the manner which was, in the 1960s, typical of the regional studies associated with *Annales*. It made considerable use of quantitative methods, to study not only fluctuations in prices and in the rates of birth, marriage and death, but also trends in the distribution of property, in agricultural productivity, and so on.

In important respects, however, *The Peasants of Languedoc* broke with tradition. As we have seen, Le Roy adopted a chronological form of organization rather than a division into 'structure' and 'conjoncture'. Within each chronological section, he discussed cultural developments such as the rise of Protestantism and literacy, and he also described the reactions of the ordinary people of his region to the economic trends they experienced in their everyday lives. In order to write this 'history from below', he drew heavily on the evidence of revolts.

For example, in the course of a discussion of the polarization of rural society in the later sixteenth century into prosperous landowners and poor wage-workers, Le Roy introduced a mini-narrative of a single episode of social conflict, in the small town of Romans. During the Carnival of 1580, craftsmen and peasants took advantage of the masquerades to proclaim that 'the rich of their town had grown wealthy at the expense of the poor', and that before long 'Christian flesh will be selling at sixpence the pound'.

Again, in his section on the economic depression of the early eighteenth century, Le Roy told the story of the guerrilla war conducted by the Camisards, the Protestant highlanders of the Cévennes, against the king who had recently outlawed their religion. He noted that the leaders of the revolt, who included young girls, were frequently seized with fits of shaking, in which they had visions of heaven and hell and prophesied events to come. Le Roy suggested that the seizures were hysterical, and he went on to relate the phenomenon to the general *conjoncture* of the period – the depression led to impoverishment, later marriage, sexual frustration, hysteria, and finally to convulsions.

Le Roy's thesis was generally well received.[108] Indeed, it made his reputation. Over the years, however, some substantial criticisms have emerged. His account of the prophets of the Cévennes, for example, has been criticized for treating them as pathological cases, rather than reading their spirit possession as an authentic form of body language.[109] His economic analysis, according to one critic, 'does not make sense' because it 'confuses rent with profit'.[110]

More fundamentally still, Le Roy's 'demographic model' of change in Languedoc has been attacked by Marxists on the grounds that it is too simply Malthusian, and that 'it is the structure of class relations, of class power, which will determine the manner and degree to which particular demographic and commercial changes will affect long-run trends in the distribution of income and economic growth, and not vice versa'. To this Le Roy has replied that his model is not simple but complex, 'neo-Malthusian', and that it incorporates the class structure.[111] We are left with two rival models of social change: a demographic model which incorporates class, and a class model which incorporates demography. As in the case of the debate over freedom and determinism around Braudel's *Mediterranean*, there seems no way of deciding the question empirically.

Whether one accepts the author's explanatory model or not, *The Peasants of Languedoc* compels admiration for its successful and unusual combination of meticulous, quantitative economic and social history with brilliantly impressionistic political, religious and psychohistory. Looking back at this study more than twenty years after its publication, it is now clear that Le Roy was one of the first to see the limitations of the Braudelian paradigm, and to work out how it should be modified. These modifications, largely the work of the third generation of *Annales*, are the subject of the next chapter.

4

The Third Generation

The rise of a third generation became more and more obvious in the years after 1968: in 1969, when young men like André Burguière and Jacques Revel became involved in the management of *Annales*; in 1972, when Braudel retired from the Presidency of the Sixth Section (which went to Jacques Le Goff); and in 1975, when the old Sixth Section disappeared and Le Goff became the president of the reorganized Ecole des Hautes Etudes en Sciences Sociales (where he was succeeded in 1977 by François Furet).

More important than the administrative changes, however, are the intellectual shifts of the last twenty years. The problem is that the intellectual portrait of the third generation is more difficult to paint than that of the first and second. No one now dominates the group as Febvre and Braudel once did. Indeed, some commentators have spoken of intellectual fragmentation.[1]

At the very least, one has to admit that polycentrism prevails. Some members of the group have been taking Lucien Febvre's programme even further, extending the frontiers of history to incorporate childhood, dreams, the body, and even smells.[2] Others have been undermining the programme, by returning to political history and the history of events. Some continue to practise quantitative history, others have reacted against it.

The third generation is the first to include women, notably Christiane Klapisch, who works on the history of the family in

Tuscany in the Middle Ages and the Renaissance; Arlette Farge, who studies the social world of the street in eighteenth-century Paris; Mona Ozouf, the author of a well-known study of festivals during the French Revolution; and Michèle Perrot, who has written on labour history and the history of women.[3] Earlier *Annales* historians have sometimes been criticized by feminists for leaving women out of history, or more exactly (since they had obviously mentioned women from time to time, from Marguerite de Navarre to the so-called witches), for missing opportunities to incorporate women more fully into history.[4] In the third generation, however, this criticism is becoming less and less valid. Indeed, Georges Duby and Michèle Perrot are involved in organizing a multi-volume history of women.

This generation is also much more open than its predecessors to ideas from outside France. Many of its members have spent a year or more in the United States – in Princeton, Ithaca, Madison, or San Diego. Unlike Braudel, they speak as well as read English. In their different ways, they have tried to make a synthesis between the *Annales* tradition and American intellectual trends – psychohistory, the new economic history, the history of popular culture, symbolic anthropology, and so on.

New approaches are still being explored by historians who identify with the *Annales* movement, as this chapter will try to show. All the same, the centre of gravity in historical writing is no longer Paris, as it surely was between the 1930s and the 1960s. Similar innovations are taking place more or less simultaneously in different parts of the globe. Women's history, for example, has been developing not only in France but also in the United States, Britain, the Netherlands, Scandinavia, West Germany, and Italy. The general history of women planned by Georges Duby and Michèle Perrot is written not for a French publisher, but for Laterza. There is more than one centre of innovation – or no centre at all.

In the pages that follow, I shall concentrate on three major themes: the rediscovery of the history of mentalities; the attempt to employ quantitative methods in cultural history; and finally, the reaction against such methods, whether it takes the form of a historical anthropology, a return to politics, or a revival of narrative. The price of this decision is unfortunately to exclude a good deal of interesting work, notably the contribution to women's history currently made by Farge, Klapisch, Perrot and others. However, concentration is the only way to prevent this chapter becoming as fragmented as the *Annales* school is said to be.

I FROM THE CELLAR TO THE ATTIC

In the Braudel generation, as we have seen, the history of mentalities and other forms of cultural history were not entirely neglected, but they were relegated to the margins of the *Annales* enterprise. In the course of the 1960s and 1970s, however, an important shift of interest took place. The intellectual itinerary of more than one *Annales* historian has led from the economic base to the cultural 'superstructure', 'from the cellar to the attic'.[5]

Why should this have happened? The shift of interest was in part, I am sure, a reaction against Braudel. It also formed a part of a much more widespread reaction against determinism of any kind.

It was actually a man of Braudel's generation who drew public attention to the history of mentalities in a remarkable, almost sensational, book he published in 1960. Philippe Ariès was an amateur historian, '*un historien de dimanche*' as he called himself, who worked at an institute for tropical fruits and devoted his leisure to historical research. Trained as a historical demographer, Ariès came to reject the quantitative approach (as he rejected other aspects of the modern industrial–bureaucratic world). His interests shifted towards the relationship between nature and culture, to the ways in which a given culture views and categorizes natural phenomena such as childhood and death.

In his study of families and schools during the old regime, Ariès argued that the idea of childhood, or more exactly the sense of childhood (*le sentiment de l'enfance*), did not exist in the Middle Ages. The age-group we call 'children' were regarded more or less like animals until the age of seven, and more or less like miniature adults thereafter. Childhood, according to Ariès, was discovered in France in the seventeenth century or thereabouts. It was at this time, for instance, that children began to be given special clothes, like the 'robe' for small boys. Letters and diaries of the period document increasing interest in children's behaviour on the part of adults, who sometimes attempted to reproduce childish speech. Ariès also drew on iconographical evidence such as the increasing numbers of portraits of children to make the case that awareness of childhood as a phase in human development goes back to the early modern period – but no further.[6]

Centuries of Childhood, as the book is known in English, is open to criticism, and it has indeed been criticized by many scholars, fairly and unfairly. Specialists in the Middle Ages have produced evidence against its sweeping generalizations about that period. Other historians have criticized Ariès for discussing European developments on the basis of evidence virtually limited to France alone, and for failing to distinguish sufficiently between the attitudes of men and women, elites and ordinary people.[7] All the same, it was the achievement of Philippe Ariès to put childhood on the historical map, to inspire hundreds of studies of the history of childhood in different regions and periods, and to draw the attention of psychologists and paediatricians to the new history.

Ariès spent the last years of his life working on attitudes to death, focusing once more on a phenomenon of nature as refracted through culture, Western culture, and responding to a famous plea of Lucien Febvre's (in 1941), 'We have no history of death.'[8] His large book, *The Hour of Our Death*, offered an account of developments over the very long term, a thousand years or so, distinguishing a sequence of five attitudes from the 'tame death' (*la mort apprivoisée*) of the earlier Middle Ages, a view defined as 'a compound of indifference, resignation, familiarity and lack of privacy', to what he calls the 'invisible death' (*la mort inversée*) of our own culture, in which, inverting the practices of the Victorians, we treat death as taboo while discussing sex openly.[9] *The Hour of Our Death* has very much the same merits and defects as the same author's *Centuries of Childhood*. There is the same boldness and originality, the same use of a wide range of evidence (including literature and art but not statistics), and the same unwillingness to chart regional or social variations.[10]

The work of Philippe Ariès was a challenge to historical demographers in particular, a challenge to which some of them responded by paying increasing attention to the role of values and mentalities in 'demographic behaviour' – in other words, by studying the history of the family, the history of sexuality, and, as Febvre had hoped, the history of love. The central figure in these developments is Jean-Louis Flandrin, whose studies of old-regime France have addressed such questions as the nature of parental authority, attitudes to small children, the influence of the Church's teachings on sexuality, and the emotional life of the peasants.[11] Studies in this area in particular have done a good deal to bridge the gap between a history of mentalities based on literary sources (Febvre's *Rabelais*, for example) and a social history without a place for attitudes and values.

Within the *Annales* group, some historians had always been concerned primarily with culture: Alphonse Dupront, for example. Dupront, another historian of Braudel's generation, has never been widely known, but his influence on younger French historians has been considerable.[12] From this point of view, he might indeed be considered the Labrousse of cultural history. His doctoral thesis, which attracted favourable attention from Braudel for its concern with unconscious attitudes, studied the idea of a 'crusade' as an instance of sacralization, a holy war to obtain possession of holy places.[13] More recently he has focused his attention on pilgrimage, viewed as a quest for the sacred and an example of 'collective sensibility' to sites of cosmic power such as Lourdes or Rocamadour. His interest in sacred space has inspired some of his pupils to investigate changes in the layout of churches and the symbolic meaning of these changes. He combines his interest in grand themes such as the sacred with precision in the inventory or cartography or (say) miraculous images. Throughout his career, Dupront has worked for rapprochements between the history of religion and psychology, sociology, and anthropology.[14]

The leading figure in historical psychology *à la* Fabvre was the late Robert Mandrou.[15] Soon after Febvre's death, Mandrou found among his papers a file of notes for an unwritten book which would have continued the study of Rabelais by considering the rise of the modern French mentality. Mandrou decided to pursue his master's enterprise and published his *Introduction to Modern France*, subtitled 'An Essay in historical psychology, 1500–1640', and including chapters on health, emotions, and mentalities.[16] Soon after the publication of this book came the breach between Mandrou and Braudel. Whatever personal reasons lay behind it, this breach took place in the course of a debate about the future of the *Annales* movement. In this debate, Braudel supported innovation, while Mandrou defended the heritage of Febvre, what he called 'the original style' (*Annales première manière*), in which historical psychology or the history of mentalities played an important part.

Mandrou pursued this approach with a book on popular culture in the seventeenth and eighteenth centuries. He continued in the same direction with a study of *Magistrates and Sorcerers in 17th-century France* (subtitled 'An analysis of historical psychology').[17] Both subjects, popular culture and witchcraft, rapidly attracted increasing historical interest at this time. Jean Delumeau, who had begun as an economic and social historian, shifted his interests from the production of alum in the papal states to problems in the history of culture. His first move was in the direction of the history of the Reformation and of the so-called 'dechristianization' of Europe. More recently, Delumeau has turned to historical psychology in Febvre's sense of the term, and written an ambitious history of fear and guilt in the West, distinguishing 'the fears of the majority' (the sea, ghosts, plague, and hunger) from the fears of 'the ruling culture' (Satan, Jews, women – and especially witches).[18]

Psychohistory   Delumeau, incidentally, made cautious use of the ideas of psychoanalysts such as Wilhelm Reich and Erik Fromm. He had been preceded in this direction by Emmanuel Le Roy Ladurie, whose *Peasants of Languedoc* (1966), discussed in the previous chapter, included works by Freud in his bibliography, sandwiched between a study of grain prices in Toulouse and an analysis of early modern class structure. Le Roy described the carnival of Romans as a psychodrama, 'giving immediate access to the creations of the unconscious', such as fantasies of cannibalism, and he interpreted the prophetic convulsions of the Camisards in terms of hysteria. As he was the first to admit, 'Cavalier and Mazel (the leaders of the revolt) cannot be invited to stretch out on the couch of some hypothetical historian–psychoanalyst. One can only note certain obvious traits that are generally encountered in similar cases of hysteria.'[19] In a similar manner, Le Roy looked at a previously neglected aspect of witchcraft trials, the accusation that witches had made their victim impotent by tying a knot during the marriage ceremony, a ritual that he interpreted persuasively as symbolic castration.[20]

Other members of the *Annales* group were moving in a similar direction, notably Alain Besançon, a specialist on nineteenth-century Russia, who wrote a long essay in *Annales* on the possibilities of what he called 'psycho-analytic history'. Besançon tried to put these possibilities into practice in a study of fathers and sons. The study focused on two tsars, Ivan the Terrible and Peter the Great, the first of whom killed his son while the second had his son put to death.[21]

Lucien Febvre had taken his ideas about psychology from Blondel and Wallon. Besançon, Le Roy Ladurie and Delumeau took theirs mainly from Freud and the Freudians or neo-Freudians. Psychohistory American style, oriented towards the study of individuals, had at last encountered French *psychologie historique*, oriented towards the study of groups, although the two trends still stopped short of synthesis.

Ideologies and the Social Imagination   However, the main trend was in a rather different direction. Two of the most distinguished recruits to the history of mentalities in the early 1960s were the medievalists Jacques Le Goff and Georges Duby.

Le Goff, for example, published a famous article in 1960 on 'Merchant's Time and Church Time in the Middle Ages'.[22] In his study of the problem of unbelief in the sixteenth century, Lucien Febvre had discussed what he called the 'floating' or 'imprecise' sense of time of a period when people often did not know their exact age and measured their day not by clocks but by the sun.[23] Le Goff refined Febvre's generalizations, themselves somewhat imprecise, and discussed the conflict between the assumptions of the clergy and those of the merchants.

His most substantial contribution to the history of mentalities, however, or to that of 'the medieval imagination' (*l'imaginaire médiéval*), as he now calls it, was made twenty years later with *The Birth of Purgatory*, a history of changing representations of the afterlife. Le Goff argued that the rise of the idea of purgatory formed part of 'the transformation of feudal Christianity', that there were connections between intellectual change and social change. At the same time he insisted on the 'mediation' of 'mental structures', 'habits of thought', or 'intellectual apparatus'; in other words, mentalities, noting the rise in the twelfth and thirteenth centuries of new attitudes to time, space, and number, including what he called 'the book-keeping of the after-life'.[24]

As for Georges Duby, he had made his reputation as an economic and social historian of medieval France. His thesis, published in 1953, dealt with society in the Macon region. It was followed by a substantial work of synthesis on the rural economy of the medieval West. These studies are very much in the tradition of Marc Bloch's *Feudal Society* and *French Rural History*. In the 1960s, as his interests gradually shifted towards mentalities, Duby collaborated with Robert Mandrou on a cultural history of France.

More recently, Duby has moved beyond Bloch and the *Annales première manière*. Inspired in part by neo-Marxian social theory, he has become concerned with the history of ideologies, cultural reproduction, and the social imagination (*l'imaginaire*), which he attempts to combine with the history of mentalities.

Duby's most important book, *The Three Orders*, runs parallel in many respects to Le Goff's *Purgatory*. It investigates what the author calls 'the relations between the material and the mental in the course of social change' by means of a case study, that of the collective representation of society as divided into three groups – priests, knights and peasants; in other words, those who pray, those who fight, and those who work (or plough – the Latin verb *laborare* is conveniently ambiguous).

Duby is well aware that, as the great classical scholar Georges Dumézil has pointed out, this view of society as composed of three groups exercising three basic functions goes back a long way into Indo-European tradition, and can be found from ancient India to Gaul in the time of Caesar. Duby argues, as medievalists had done before, that this image of three orders performed the function of legitimating the exploitation of the peasants by their lords by suggesting that all three groups served society in their different ways.

He does not stop there, however. What interests him is the reason for the reactivation of this conception of the tripartite society, from Wessex to Poland, from the ninth century onwards, and he devotes a long discussion to the social and political context of this revival, particularly in France, where the image re-emerged in the early eleventh century.

Duby suggests that the reactivation of the image corresponded to a new need. At a time of political crisis, in eleventh-century France, for example, it was a 'weapon' in the hands of monarchs, who claimed to concentrate the three basic functions in their own person. Latent in the 'mentality' of the time, this intellectual system was made manifest as ideology for political ends. Ideology, remarks Duby, is not a passive reflection of society, but a plan for acting upon it.[25]

Duby's conception of ideology is not far from that of the philosopher Louis Althusser, who once defined it as 'the imaginary [or imagined] relation of individuals to their real conditions of existence' (*le rapport imaginaire des individus à leurs conditions réelles d'existence*).[26] In similar fashion to Duby, a specialist on the eighteenth century, Michel Vovelle has made a serious attempt to fuse the history of *mentalités collectives*, in the style of Febvre and

Lefebvre, with the Marxian history of ideologies.[27]

It is scarcely surprising to find important contributions to the history of mentalities being made by medievalists such as Duby and Le Goff. The remoteness from us of the Middle Ages, their 'otherness', poses a problem that an approach of this type helps to resolve. On the other hand, the kinds of source surviving from the Middle Ages make the period somewhat less amenable to another of the new approaches to culture, serial history.

II   THE 'THIRD LEVEL' OF SERIAL HISTORY

The history of mentalities was not pushed to the periphery of *Annales* in its second generation simply because Braudel was not interested in it. There were at least two more important reasons for its marginalization at this time. In the first place, a good many French historians believed – or at any rate assumed – that economic and social history was more important, or more fundamental, than other aspects of the past. In the second place, the new quantitative approaches discussed in the previous chapter could not get a purchase on mentalities as easily as they could on the economic and social structure.

The first of these approaches to cultural history is the quantitative or serial approach, along the lines suggested by Pierre Chaunu in a well-known manifesto for what he called (following a remark by Ernest Labrousse) 'the quantitative at the third level'.[28] Lucien Febvre's article 'Amiens: From the Renaissance to the Counter-Reformation', published in *Annales* in 1941, showed the value of studying a series of documents (in his case inventories post mortem) over the long term, in order to chart changes in attitudes and even in artistic taste.[29] However, Febvre did not offer his readers precise statistics. The statistical approach was developed to study the history of religious practice, the history of the book, and the history of literacy. It spread to other domains of cultural history somewhat later.

The idea of a history of French religious practice, or a retrospective sociology of French Catholicism based on statistics for attendance at communion, vocations to the priesthood, etc., goes back to Gabriel Le Bras, who published an article on the subject as early as 1931.[30] Le Bras, a Catholic priest and one of Febvre's and Bloch's colleagues at Strasbourg, had broad interests in theology, history, law, and sociology. He founded a school of church historians and sociologists of religion who were particularly concerned with what they called the problem of 'dechristianization' in France from the late eighteenth century onwards, and investigated this problem by means of quantitative methods.

Le Bras and his followers did not form part of the *Annales* group – they were generally priests, and they had their own network of centres and journals such as the *Revue de l'histoire de l'église de France*. However, the work of Le Bras (which was warmly welcomed by his former colleague Lucien Febvre) and his followers was clearly inspired by the *Annales*.[31] As an example of this substantial body of work, one might take a thesis on the diocese of La Rochelle in the seventeenth and eighteenth centuries. It is organized in much the same way as one of the regional studies associated with *Annales*, beginning with the geography of the diocese, on the frontier between the plain and the *bocage*, moving on to discuss the religious situation, and ending with events and trends from 1648 to 1724. The use of quantitative methods also recalls the regional monographs by the disciples of Braudel and Labrousse.[32]

In turn, the work of the Le Bras circle (like that of Ariès) inspired the work of some *Annales* historians as they climbed from the cellar to the attic. Recent regional studies (dealing with Anjou, Provence, Avignon, and Brittany) have focused more sharply on culture than their predecessors, and in particular on attitudes to death. As Le Goff put it in the preface to one of these studies, 'death is in fashion' (*la mort est à la mode*).[33]

The most original of these studies is Vovelle's. A Marxist historian of the French Revolution, 'formed in the school of Ernest Labrousse' as he puts it, Michel Vovelle became interested in the problem of 'dechristianization'. He thought of trying to measure this process by means of the study of attitudes to death and the beyond as revealed by wills. The result, written up in his doctoral thesis, was a study of Provence on the basis of a systematic analysis of some 30,000 testaments. Where earlier historians had juxtaposed quantitative evidence about mortality with more literary evidence about attitudes to death, Vovelle attempted to measure changes in thought and feeling. He paid attention, for example, to references to the protection of patron saints; the numbers of masses that the testator wanted to be said for the repose of his or her soul; the arrangements for funerals, and even the weight of the candles used during the ceremony.

Vovelle identified a major shift from what he called the 'baroque pomp' of seventeenth-century funerals to the modesty of their eighteenth-century counterparts. His main assumption was that the language of wills reflected 'the system of collective representations', and his main conclusion was the identification of a trend towards secularization, suggesting that the 'dechristianization' of the years of the French Revolution was spontaneous rather than imposed from above, and that it formed part of a larger trend. Particularly noteworthy is the way in which Vovelle charted the spread of new attitudes from the nobility to the artisans and peasants, and from large towns such as Aix, Marseilles, and Toulon, through small towns such as Barcelonette to the villages. His arguments were illustrated by abundant maps, graphs, and tables.

Baroque Piety and Dechristianization, as Vovelle's study is called, caused something of an intellectual sensation, thanks in particular to its virtuoso use of statistics, controlled by an acute sense of the difficulties of interpreting them. It was this book that inspired Pierre Chaunu to organize a collective investigation of attitudes to death in Paris in the early modern period, using similar methods.[34] What Ariès was doing singlehanded on the history of death, in his deliberately impressionistic way, was thus complemented by the collective and quantitative researches of the professionals.[35]

This appropriation of the afterlife by lay historians armed with computers remains the most remarkable example of serial history at the third level. However, other historians of culture have also made effective use of quantitative methods, notably for the history of literacy and the history of the book.

The study of literacy is another domain of cultural history which lends itself to collective research and to statistical analysis. Indeed, a French headmaster had carried out research in this area in the 1870s, using signatures to marriage registers as his source, and noting the great variations between the figures for different départements, as well as the rise of literacy from the late seventeenth century onwards. In the 1950s, two historians reanalysed his data and presented in cartographic form the dramatic contrast between two Frances, separated by a line from St Malo to Geneva. North-east of this line, literacy was relatively high, south-west of the line it was low.[36]

The most important project in this domain, begun in the early 1970s, was carried out at the Ecole des Hautes Etudes and was directed by François Furet (a pupil of Ernest Labrousse who had previously worked on the quantitative analysis of social structures) and Jacques Ozouf. The project dealt with changing levels of literacy in France from the sixteenth to the nineteenth centuries.[37] The researchers drew on a wider range of sources than before, from the census to the army's statistics on conscripts, and so they were able to argue rather than assume the relationship between the ability to sign one's name and the ability to read and write. They confirmed the traditional distinction between the two Frances, but refined the analysis by considering variations within départements. Among other interesting conclusions, they noted that in the eighteenth century, literacy spread faster among women than it did among men.

Research on literacy was accompanied by research on what the French call 'the history of the book', research that focuses not on great works but on trends in book production and on the reading habits of different social groups.[38] For example, Robert Mandrou's study of popular culture, already mentioned, was concerned with chap-books, the so-called 'Blue Library' (*la Bibliothèque Bleue*, given this name because the books had covers made of the blue paper used for packing sugar).[39] These books, which cost only one or two sous, were distributed by pedlars (*colporteurs*) and they were produced in the main by a few families of printers at Troyes in north-eastern France, where the literacy rate was highest. Mandrou examined a sample of some 450 titles, noting the importance of pious reading (120 works), almanacs, and even romances of chivalry. He concluded that this was essentially an 'escapist literature', that it was read mainly by peasants, and that it revealed a 'conformist' mentality (the last two conclusions have been rejected by other scholars working in this field).

At much the same time as Mandrou, the Sixth Section launched a project for collective research on the social history of the book in eighteenth-century France.[40] However, the key figure in book history is another of Febvre's collaborators, Henri-Jean Martin of the Bibliothèque Nationale. Martin worked with Febvre on a general survey of the invention and spread of printing, *The Coming of the Book* (1958). He went on to write a rigorously quantitative study of the book trade and the reading public in seventeenth-century France. This analysed not only trends in book production, but also the changing tastes of different groups of the reading public, notably the magistrates of the Parlement of Paris, as revealed by the proportions of books on different subjects to be found in their private libraries.[41] Martin has since directed a massive collective work on the history of the book in France.[42]

One of the leading collaborators in these collective enterprises, Daniel Roche, organized a research team of his own in the mid-1970s to study the everyday life of ordinary people in eighteenth-century Paris. In the book that emerged from this collective research, *The People of Paris* (1981), a substantial chapter was devoted to popular reading, concluding that reading and writing played an important part in the lives of some groups within the lower classes, servants in particular.[43] The most striking feature of *The People of Paris*, however, was its location of this analysis of reading within the framework of a general study of the material culture of ordinary Parisians. This is a study in serial history based essentially on inventories post mortem, full of details about the clothes and furniture of the deceased, details that Roche interprets with great skill to build up a picture of everyday life. More recently still, he has written a social history of clothing in early modern France, once again combining his interests in historical anthropology, characteristic of the third generation, with the more rigorous methods of his old master, Ernest Labrousse.[44]

III   REACTIONS: ANTHROPOLOGY, POLITICS, NARRATIVE

The quantitative approach to history in general, and the quantitative approach to cultural history in particular, can obviously be criticized as reductionist. Generally speaking, what can be measured is not what matters. Quantitative historians can count signatures to marriage registers, books in private libraries, Easter communicants, references to the court of heaven, and so on. The problem remains whether these statistics are reliable indicators of literacy, piety, or whatever the historian wants to investigate. Some historians have argued the case for the reliability of their figures; others assumed it. Some have made use of other types of evidence to make their statistics meaningful, others have not. Some have remembered that they are dealing with real people, others appear to have forgotten it. Any evaluation of the movement must discriminate between the modest and the extreme claims made for the method and also between the manners in which it has been employed, crudely or with finesse.

By the later 1970s, the dangers of this kind of history had become apparent. Indeed, there was something of an undiscriminating backlash against the quantitative approach. At much the same time there was a more general reaction against much of what *Annales* stood for , in particular against the dominance of both social and structural history. Looking at the positive side of these reactions, we may distinguish three trends: an anthropological turn, a return to politics, and a revival of narrative.

The Anthropological Turn   The anthropological turn might be described with more exactitude as a turn towards cultural or 'symbolic' anthropology. After all, Bloch and Febvre had read their Frazer and their Lévy-Bruhl, and made use of this reading in their work on medieval and sixteenth-century mentalities. Braudel was familiar with the work of Marcel Mauss, which underlies his discussion of cultural frontiers and exchanges. In the 1960s, Duby had drawn on the work of Mauss and Malinowski on the function of gifts in order to understand the economic history of the early Middle Ages.[45]

All earlier historians seem to have wanted from their neighbour discipline was the opportunity to raid it from time to time in search of new concepts. Some historians of the 1970s and 1980s, however, harbour rather more serious intentions. They may even think in terms of marriage, in other words of 'historical anthropology' or 'anthropological history' (*ethnohistoire*).[46]

What attracts these historians is above all the new 'symbolic anthropology'. The names that recur in their footnotes include Erving Goffman and Victor Turner (both of whom stress the dramaturgical elements in everyday life), Pierre Bourdieu, and Michel De Certeau. Bourdieu, who has shifted from anthropological studies of Algeria to the sociology of contemporary France, has been influential in many ways. His ideas on the sociology of education (one of his main areas of interest), especially the idea of education as a means of 'social reproduction', have informed recent studies on the social history of schools and universities.[47] His notion of 'symbolic capital' underlies some recent work on the history of conspicuous consumption. Historians of mentalities, popular culture and everyday life have all learned from Bourdieu's 'theory of practice'. His replacement of the idea of social 'rules' (which he considers too rigid and determinist) by more flexible concepts such as 'strategy' and 'habitus' has affected the practice of French historians so pervasively that it would be misleading to reduce it to specific examples (such as the matrimonial strategies of nobles in the Middle Ages).[48]

Another pervasive influence is the late Michel De Certeau. De Certeau was a Jesuit who specialized in the history of religion. However, it was impossible to tie him down to any one discipline. He was, among other things, a psychoanalyst, and his discussion of seventeenth-century cases of diabolical possession was original and important.[49] Even more influential were his contributions in three other fields. Together with two historians from the *Annales* group, De Certeau wrote a pioneering study of the politics of language, focusing on an enquiry into patois conducted during the French Revolution and reflecting the regime's desire for uniformity and centralization.[50] He also organized a collective study of contemporary French daily life in which he rejected the myth of the passive consumer and stressed what he called 'consumption as production'; in other words, the creativity of ordinary people in adapting mass-produced artefacts (from furniture to television dramas) to their personal needs.[51] Most important of all, perhaps, were his essays on the writing of history, concentrating on the process that he described as the construction of 'the other' (the Indians of Brazil, for example), often as the inverse of the writer's image of himself.[52]

The ideas of Goffman, Turner, Bourdieu, De Certeau and others have been adopted, adapted, and utilized for the construction of a more anthropological history. Jacques Le Goff, for example, has been working for some twenty years on what might be described as the cultural anthropology of the Middle Ages, ranging from the structural analysis of medieval legends to the study of symbolic gestures in social life, notably the ritual of vassalage.[53] Emmanuel Le Roy Ladurie has moved in the same direction in a series of studies, of which the most famous by far is his *Montaillou*.[54]

Montaillou is a village in the Ariège in south-west France, a region in which the Cathar heresy had considerable appeal at the beginning of the fourteenth century. The heretics were pursued, interrogated and punished by the local bishop, Jacques Fournier. The register of the interrogations has survived, and it was published in 1965. It was doubtless Le Roy's interest in social anthropology that allowed him to see the value of this source, not just for the study of the Cathars but for French rural history. He noticed that twenty-five individuals, about a quarter of the suspects named in the register, came from a single village. His inspiration was to treat the register as the record of a set of interviews with these twenty-five people (about 10 per cent of the population of the village). All he had to do, Le Roy tells us, was to rearrange the information given by the suspects to the inquisitors in the form of a community study of the kind anthropologists have so often written.[55] He divided it into two parts. The first deals with the material culture of Montaillou, the houses, for example, built of stone without mortar, allowing neighbours to observe and to listen to one another through the chinks. The second part of the book is concerned with the mentalities of the villagers – their sense of time and space, childhood and death, sexuality, God, and nature.

Like Braudel, Le Roy describes and analyses Mediterranean culture and society, but no one could say that he has left the people out of his book. It has attracted a huge readership, and it remains in the memory essentially because the author has the gift to bring individuals back to life, from the gentle, freedom-loving Pierre Maury, 'the good shepherd', to the local noble-woman, the sexy Béatrice des Planissoles, and her seducer, the aggressive and self-confident priest, Pierre Clergue.

Montaillou is also an ambitious study of social and cultural history. Its originality does not lie in the questions it addresses, which, as we have seen, are the questions that have been asked by two generations of French historians, including Febvre (on unbelief), Braudel (on the house), Ariès (on childhood), Flandrin (on sexuality), and so on. Le Roy was one of the first to use inquisition registers for the reconstruction of everyday life and attitudes, but he was not alone in this. The novelty of his approach lies in his attempt to write a historical community study in the anthropological sense – not a history of a particular village, but a portrait of the village, told in the words of the inhabitants themselves, and a portrait of a larger society, which the villagers represent. *Montaillou* is an early example of what has come to be called 'microhistory'.[56] The author has studied the world in a grain of sand, or, in his own metaphor, the ocean through a drop of liquid.

It is on this very point that some of the most serious criticisms of the book have concentrated.[57] *Montaillou* has been faulted (apart from inaccuracies of detail) for an insufficiently critical use of its main source, which Le Roy once described as 'the unmediated testimony of the peasants about themselves' (*le témoignage sans intermédiaire, que porte le paysan sur lui-meme*).[58] It is of course nothing of the kind. The villagers gave their evidence in Occitan and it was taken down in Latin. They were not spontaneously talking about themselves, but replying to questions under threat of torture. Historians cannot afford to forget these intermediaries between themselves and the men and women they study.

The second main criticism of the book – and of the increasingly popular microhistorical approach that it has helped to inspire – raises the question of typicality. No community is an island, not even a mountain village such as Montaillou. Its connections with the outside world, as far away as Catalonia, emerge clearly in the book itself. The question remains: What larger unit does the village represent? Of what ocean is it a drop? Is it supposed to be typical of the Ariège, the south of France, the Mediterranean world, or the Middle Ages? Despite his previous experience with statistics and samples, the author fails to discuss this crucial problem of method. Could this be because he wrote *Montaillou* in reaction against the aridities of quantitative history?

As in the case of the stone houses of the village itself, it is easy to pick holes in *Montaillou*. It deserves to be remembered above all for its author's power of bringing the past to life, and also for putting the documents to the question, reading them between the lines, and making them reveal what the villagers did not even know they knew. It is a brilliant *tour de force* of the historical imagination, and a revelation of the possibilities of an anthropological history.

More paradoxical is the contribution to such a history made by Roger Chartier, who is best known for his work on the history of the book in association with Martin, Roche and others discussed in the preceding section. It may well seem odd to describe a specialist in the history of literacy as a historical anthropologist, and I am far from sure that Chartier would accept this label.[59] All the same, the thrust of his work is in the same direction as recent work in cultural anthropology.

The importance of Chartier's essays is that they both exemplify and discuss a shift in approach, as he puts it himself, 'from the social history of culture to the cultural history of society'. That is, the essays suggest that what earlier historians inside and outside the *Annales* tradition generally assumed to be objective structures need to be viewed as culturally 'constituted' or 'constructed'. Society itself is a collective representation.

The studies of mentalities by Philippe Ariès implied that childhood and death were cultural constructs, but in the work of Roger Chartier this point becomes explicit. He chooses to study not so much peasants or vagabonds as upper-class views of peasants or vagabonds, images of 'the other'.[60] Unlike Furet and Ozouf (above), he does not discuss the objective differences between France north-east and south-west of the line from St Malo to Geneva. He concentrates on the idea of the 'two Frances', its history, and the effects of this stereotype on government policies.[61] In taking his distance from so-called 'objective' factors, Chartier is in step with current anthropology, with recent work on 'the imaginary' (discussed above), and also with the late Michel Foucault.

Despite Foucault's critique of the idea of 'influence', it is difficult not to use the term to describe the effects of his books on French historians of the *Annales* group. It was thanks to him that they discovered the history of the body and the links between that history and the history of power. Also important in the intellectual development of many of the third generation was Foucault's critique of historians for what he called their 'meagre idea of the real'; in other words, their reduction of the real to the domain of the social, leaving out thought. The recent turn towards the 'cultural history of society', well exemplified by Chartier, owes much to Foucault's work.[62]

Chartier's studies of the history of the book follow similar lines and show his increasing dissatisfaction with the history of mentalities and with serial history at the third level.[63] His essays on the Bibliothèque Bleue, for example, undermine the interpretation offered by Robert Mandrou (and discussed above), by suggesting that these chap-books were not read exclusively by the peasants, or indeed by ordinary people. Before 1660, at least, the customers were generally Parisians.[64]

A more general point on which Chartier insists is that it is impossible 'to establish exclusive relationships between specific cultural forms and particular social groups'. This of course makes the serial history of culture a good deal more difficult, if not completely impossible. Chartier has therefore shifted his attention, following Pierre Bourdieu and Michel De Certeau, to cultural 'practices' shared by various groups.[65]

In his own analysis of chap-books and other texts, the central term is 'appropriation'. The popular must not, he suggests, be identified with a particular corpus of texts, objects, beliefs or whatever. It resides in 'a way of using cultural products', such as printed matter or festivals. Chartier's essays are therefore largely concerned with rewriting, with the transformations undergone by particular texts, as they were adapted to the needs of the public, or more exactly of successive publics.

A similar concern for appropriation and transformation underlies one of the most impressive French historical enterprises of recent years, the collective work on *The Places of Memory* edited by Pierre Nora, who combines the roles of publisher and historian.[66] These volumes, which discuss themes such as the tricolour, the 'Marseillaise', the Pantheon, and the image of the past to be found in encyclopaedias and school textbooks, mark a return to the ideas of Maurice Halbwachs on the social framework of memory, ideas that had inspired Marc Bloch but had been rather neglected by later historians. In their concern for the uses of the past for the present, they exemplify an anthropological approach: a reflexive anthropology in this case, since the authors are a group of French historians writing about French history. Organized around the themes of 'the Revolution' and 'the Nation', these volumes also reveal a return to politics.

The Return to Politics[67] Perhaps the most notorious charge against the so-called *Annales* school has been their supposed neglect of politics, a charge to which the journal seems to confess by carrying on its masthead the slogan '*economies sociétés civilisations*' with no mention of states. There is indeed some substance in the criticism, but it is necessary to make it more precise.

Febvre and Braudel may have concentrated their efforts on academic politics, but a number of the leading historians of the group were involved in the politics of post-war France, often as members – at least for a time – of the Communist Party. The reminiscences of one of them give a vivid picture of the party meetings, the denunciations, expulsions, and resignations of the years following 1956.[68]

The charge of neglecting politics was of course directed against the historical work of the group, but here too nuances are needed. It would be difficult, for instance, to substain the argument in the case of Marc Bloch. His *Royal Touch* was intended as a contribution to the history of ideas of kingship. His *Feudal Society* begins with an account of the Viking, Muslim and Hungarian invasions of Western Europe, and includes a long section on feudalism as a form of government.

In the case of Lucien Febvre, the charge has more substance. Although he had discussed the Revolt of the Netherlands at considerable length in his thesis on Philip II and Franche-Comté, Febvre later denounced political history with his customary violence, and turned to religion and mentalities. In the case of Braudel, it should be noted that the structural section of *The Mediterranean* includes chapters on empires and the organization of war. It is the history of political and military events that he dismisses as the most superficial kind of history.

The regional studies of early modern France that bear the imprint of *Annales* have generally confined themselves to economic and social history. Goubert's *Beauvais* is an obvious example. Yet no one can label Goubert an unpolitical historian. He went on to write a book on Louis XIV and a study of the old regime of which the second volume is concerned with power.[69] Perhaps the region is not the appropriate framework for a study of old-regime politics. Such an assumption may well have deterred the authors of some regional studies from including a section on politics. However, the work of Mousnier's pupils on popular revolt, together with some recent American studies of politics at a regional level, suggest that the assumption was mistaken and that a splendid opportunity for 'total history' was lost.[70] The obvious exception to the rule, as we have seen, is Le Roy Ladurie, who did discuss revolts in Languedoc (if not the administration of the province), and who has since produced some explicitly political studies.[71]

The medievalists in the *Annales* group are far from dismissing political history, even if they devote more attention to other topics. Georges Duby, who began as an economic and social historian and shifted to the history of mentalities, has written a monograph on a medieval battle, Bouvines (to be discussed below). His account of the genesis or reactivation of the idea of the three estates places this idea in a political context, the crisis of the French and other monarchies. Jacques Le Goff considers that politics is no longer the 'backbone' of history in the sense that 'it cannot aspire to autonomy'.[72] However, he shares Bloch's interest in sacred kingship and he is now at work on a study of a medieval ruler.

It is scarcely surprising, however, to find that most attention to politics has been paid by the historians in the *Annales* group who concern themselves with what the French call 'contemporary history'; in other words, with the period that began in 1789. François Furet and Michel Vovelle, who have devoted much of their time to the French Revolution (despite their other historical interests) cannot be accused of neglecting politics. Nor can Marc Ferro, historian of the Russian Revolution and the First World War. However, the outstanding figure in this domain is surely Maurice Agulhon.

Agulhon is the author of *The Republic in the Village*, a study of the political behaviour of ordinary people in the Var (in Provence) from 1789 to 1851.[73] This study employs a broadly Marxist framework, that of the growth of political consciousness. The years 1815–48 are described as the years of preparation, in which conflicts over encroachments on common rights (notably over forest timber), together with the 'widening of cultural horizons' following the spread of literacy, encouraged the growth of political consciousness in the region. The brief years of the Second Republic, 1848–51, are presented as the years of 'revelation', in which the ordinary people of the Var voted for the first time and voted for the Left.

Although it deals more with the countryside than with towns, it is tempting to describe Agulhon's study as concerned with 'the making of the Provençal working class'.[74] The parallel with Edward Thompson can be extended. Both historians were 'open', empiricist, eclectic Marxists.[75] Both were concerned with forms of 'sociability'. Thompson discussed friendly societies and their 'rituals of mutuality'.[76] Agulhon, thanks to whom the word *sociabilité* is now current coinage in France, had studied masonic lodges and Catholic confraternities from this point of view, and went on to study the bourgeois 'circle' and the café. Both historians took culture seriously. Thompson described the tradition of popular radicalism; Agulhon described charivaris and carnivals, such as the 'seditious carnival' of Vidauban in 1850, mild enough if compared to the Carnival of Romans in 1580, but significant as an illustration of the opposed but complementary processes of 'archaism' and modernity, the 'folklorization' of politics and the politicization of folklore.[77]

There is a similarly fruitful interpenetration of political and cultural history in Agulhon's more recent work. His *Marianne into Battle* analyses French republican imagery and symbolism from 1789 to 1880, focusing on representations of Marianne, the personification of the Republic, and emphasizing the changing meaning of her image – in popular culture as well as in elite culture – between the Revolution and the Commune.[78] His essay in *The Places of Memory* follows similar lines, and presents the nineteenth-century town hall (*la mairie*) as an embodiment of republican values, a text that the historian needs to learn to read.[79]

To sum up. Febvre and Braudel may not have ignored political history, but they did not make it their highest priority. The return to politics in the third generation is a reaction against Braudel, and also against other forms of determinism (notably Marxist 'economism'). It is associated with a rediscovery of the importance of agency as opposed to structure. It is also associated with a sense of the importance of what the Americans call 'political culture', of ideas and mentalities. Thanks to Foucault, it has also been extended in the direction of 'micropolitics', the struggle for power in the family, in schools, in factories, and so on.[80] As a result of these changes, political history is in the course of renewal.[81]

The Revival of Narrative   The return to political history is linked to the reaction against determinism which also inspired the anthropological turn, as we have seen. The concern with human freedom (together with the interest in microhistory) also underlies the recent revival of historical biography, inside and outside the *Annales*. Georges Duby has published a biography of a medieval Englishman, William the Marshal, while Jacques Le Goff is at work on the life of a king of France, St Louis. The revival is not a simple return to the past. Historical biography is practised for different reasons and it takes different forms. It can be a means to understand the mentality of a group. One of the forms it takes is the life of a more or less ordinary person, like the bourgeois of Aix-en-Provence, Joseph Sec, on whose 'irresistible rise' Michel Vovelle has written, or the Paris craftsman, Jean-Louis Ménétra, studied by Daniel Roche.[82]

The return to politics is also associated with a revival of interest in the narrative of events. Events are not always political – think of the Great Crash of 1929, the great plague of 1348, or indeed of the publication of *War and Peace*. All the same, discussions of political history, the history of events, and historical narrative are closely intertwined. Parallel to the so-called 'return to politics', there has recently been a 'revival of narrative' among historians in France and elsewhere. The phrase is that of the British historian Lawrence Stone, who ascribes the trend to 'a widespread disillusionment with the economic determinist model of historical explanation' employed by Marxist and *Annales* historians alike, and especially with its relegation of culture to the superstructure or 'third level'.[83] There can be little doubt that Stone has perceived a significant trend, but once again nuances are in order.

The contemptuous dismissal of 'the history of events' (*histoire événementielle*) by Durkheim, Simiand and Lacombe was discussed in the overture to this book. Febvre's stress on problem-oriented history suggests that he shared this view, despite the place given to the events of the Revolt of the Netherlands in his doctoral thesis. Marc Bloch, so far as I know, never denounced the history of events, but never wrote that kind of history either.

As for Braudel, he both denounced it and wrote it. More exactly, as we have seen, he declared the history of events to be the surface of history. He did not say that this surface was uninteresting – on the contrary, he described it as 'the most exciting of all'.[84] Its interest for him, however, was in what it might reveal about the 'deeper realities', the currents below the surface. For Braudel, events were simply mirrors reflecting the history of structures. In his magisterial study of time and narrative, the philosopher Paul Ricoeur has argued that all works of history are narratives, even Braudel's *Mediterranean*. His demonstration of similarities between conventional and structural histories (in their temporality, their causality, and so on) is difficult to rebut. All the same, to call *The Mediterranean* a narrative history is surely to employ the term 'narrative' in such a broad sense that it loses its usefulness.[85]

Most of the regional monographs of the 1960s and 1970s went further than Braudel in this direction in the sense that they included no narrative at all. The exception was Le Roy Ladurie's *Peasants of Languedoc*, in which, as we have seen, structural analysis alternated with accounts of events, notably protests: the Carnival of Romans in 1580, the rising in the Vivarais in 1670, the revolt of the Camisards in 1702.

Le Roy's treatment of events as reactions or responses to structural change was not far from Braudel's view of events as mirrors or as litmus papers revealing underlying structures. A similar point might be made about a book which Georges Duby published in 1973, a book that might well have shocked Febvre, since it dealt not only with an event but with a battle, the battle of Bouvines on 27 July 1214. The book was indeed written for a rather old-fashioned series, entitled 'days which made France' (*journées qui ont fait la France*) and aimed at the general public. All the same, Duby did not return to old-fashioned history. He used contemporary accounts of the battle to illuminate medieval attitudes to war, and he discussed later views of Bouvines as a 'myth' revealing more about the narrators than the event they narrated.[86]

The obvious question that these studies do not raise is whether some events at least might not modify structures, rather than simply reflect them. What about the events of 1789, say, or 1917? The sociologist Emile Durkheim, to whom the critics of *histoire événementielle* owe so much, was prepared to dismiss even 1789 as a symptom rather than a cause of social change.[87] There are, however, signs of a shift away from this extreme Durkheimian or Braudelian position. For example, a sociological study of an area in western France, the département of the Sarthe, has argued the need to take the events of 1789 and their aftermath into account in any attempt to explain the political attitudes of the region (divided into a Left-wing east and a Right-wing west).[88]

Le Roy Ladurie has drawn attention to the implications of this study in an essay discussing what he variously calls the 'traumatic' event, the event as 'catalyst', and the 'creative event' (*l'événement-matrice*). His use of such divergent metaphors suggests that he had not made up his mind about the importance of events, and his article went no further than a general recommendation to the historian to reflect on the relation between events and structures.[89] Some years later, however, Le Roy returned to the Carnival of Romans and made it the subject of a book. He analysed the event as a 'social drama' which made manifest the conflicts latent in that small town and the country-side around it. In other words, symptom rather than cause.[90]

Of course the Carnival of Romans was not a great event. It is more difficult to dismiss as mere reflections of social structures the events of 1789, say, or the Great War of 1914–18, or the Revolution of 1917 (all topics on which *Annales* historians have written).[91] In a recent study, François Furet goes so far as to suggest not only that the events of the Revolution broke the old structures and gave France her political 'patrimony', but even that a few months of 1789 were decisive.[92]

One more feature of the third generation of *Annales* deserves our attention. It is in their time that their kind of history has become popular in France. Braudel's *Mediterranean* and the works of Bloch and Febvre did not sell many copies when they were first published. Only in 1985, when sales reached 8,500 copies, could *The Mediterranean* be described as a best-seller. *Montaillou*, on the other hand, went to the top of the non-fiction best-seller list in France, its sales boosted when Mitterand admitted on television that he had been reading it, while the village itself was almost buried under the mass of tourists.

Montaillou was a book written at the right place and the right time, carried along by the waves of ecology and regionalism, but its success is only the most spectacular example of the interest now shown by the French public in the 'new history'. When Braudel's trilogy, *Civilization and Capitalism*, was published in 1979, it received attention in the media on an altogether different scale from his earlier books. Some members of the *Annales* group appear regularly in television and radio programmes and even produce them, notably Georges Duby and Jacques Le Goff. Others, such as Pierre Chaunu, Roger Chartier, Mona Ozouf and Michèle Perrot, write on a regular basis for newspapers and journals, including *Le Figaro*, *Le Monde*, *L'Express* and *Le Nouvel Observateur*. It is difficult to think of any other country or any other period in which so many professional historians were so firmly established in the media of communication.

The writings of the *Annales* historians used to be large volumes appearing in small editions from Armand Colin (the faithful publishers of the journal) or from the Hautes Etudes themselves. Nowadays they are more likely to be slim volumes appearing in larger print runs from leading commercial publishers, often in a series edited by other *Annales* historians. In the 1960s, Ariès and Mandrou edited a series on 'Civilizations and Mentalities' for Plon. Agulhon now edits a historical series for Aubier Montaigne, while Duby has edited more than one for Seuil (including multi-volume histories of rural France, urban France, and private life). An example of still closer collaboration between historians and publishers is offered by Pierre Nora, who teaches at the Hautes Etudes as well as working for Gallimard. It was Nora who founded the well-known series *Bibliothèque des Histoires*, which includes a number of studies by his colleagues.

I am not suggesting that the media have created the wave of interest in this kind of history, though they may well have encouraged it. The producers and publishers must have thought there was a demand for history in general, and in particular for socio-cultural history, *Annales* style. This demand is not confined to France. It is time to examine the reception that the *Annales* historians have had outside their own country and discipline.

5

The *Annales* in Global Perspective

I THE RECEPTION OF *ANNALES*

It is time to examine the career of the *Annales* movement beyond
the frontiers – not only the frontiers of France but those of the
discipline of history as well. The story to be told – briefly – here
will not be a simple account of the spreading of the gospel
abroad. In fact, *Annales* has had a somewhat hostile reception in
some places. My aim is rather to describe the variety of responses
to the new history, not only praise and criticism but attempts to
put the *Annales* tools to work in different areas, attempts that
may on occasion reveal weaknesses in the original conceptions.[1]
Given the ground to be covered, this description will inevitably
be selective and impressionistic.

Annales Abroad   Before the Second World War, the *Annales*
already had allies and sympathizers abroad, from Henri Pirenne
in Belgium to R. H. Tawney in Britain.[2] All the same, it was only
in the age of Braudel that the journal and the movement became
widely known in Europe.[3]

   The Mediterranean naturally appealed to readers in that part of
the world; the Italian translation of Braudel's book appeared
(like the Spanish translation) in 1953. Two Italians, Ruggiero
Romano and Alberto Tenenti, were among Braudel's closest
collaborators. Some leading Italian historians of the 1950s were

friends of Lucien Febvre and sympathetic to the *Annales* move-ment. They ranged from Armando Sapori, historian of medieval Italian merchants, to Delio Cantimori, who shared Febvre's interest in sixteenth-century heretics. The massive *History of Italy*, launched by the publisher Giulio Einaudi in 1972, focused on developments over the long term, paid homage to Bloch in the title of the first volume, and included a long essay by Braudel.[4]

In Poland, despite the official dominance of Marxism (or maybe because of it), historians have long shown considerable enthusiasm for *Annales*. There was a tradition of interest in economic and social history in pre-war Polish universities. Jan Rutkowski wrote for *Annales* in the 1930s and founded a similar journal of his own. A substantial number of Polish historians have studied in Paris – Bronislaw Geremek, for example, a distinguished medievalist well known in the profession for his studies of the urban poor, and still more widely known as the counsellor of Lech Walesa. The Poles have shown considerable interest in the history of mentalities. *The Mediterranean* has been translated into Polish, and it has inspired a Polish study of the Baltic, published by the Centre de Recherches Historiques in their series 'Cahiers des Annales'.[5]

Still more interest was evoked by Braudel's famous essay on 'history and social sciences'.[6] Its effects can be seen in one of the most remarkable works of history to have been published in post-war Poland, the *Economic Theory of the Feudal System* (1962), by Witold Kula, a historian whom Braudel once paid the compli-ment of describing him as 'much more intelligent than I am'.[7] Kula made an economic analysis of the Polish latifundia of the seventeenth and eighteenth centuries. He pointed out that the economic behaviour of the Polish landowners was the opposite of that predicted by classical economics. When the price of rye, their major product, went up, they produced less, and when the price went down, they produced more. The explanation of the paradox has to be sought, says Kula (contrary to Braudel but in tune with other *Annales* historians) in the realm of culture, or mentality. These aristocrats were not interested in profit but in maintaining their style of life in the manner to which they had become accustomed. The variations in production were attempts to maintain a steady income. It would have been interesting to observe the reactions of Karl Marx to these ideas.[8]

In Germany, on the other hand, political history remained dominant in the 1950s and 1960s. Given the importance of new German approaches to history in the age of Schmoller, Weber and Lamprecht, discussed in the 'overture' to this study, this dominance may seem strange. However, after the traumatic experiences of 1914–18 and of 1933–45, it was hard to deny the importance of either politics or events, and the major historical controversies did indeed concentrate on Hitler and the German role in two world wars. It was only after the post-war generation had come to maturity in the 1970s that interest shifted, towards the 'history of the everyday' (*Alltagsgeschichte*), the history of popular culture, and the history of mentalities.[9]

Britain too, at least in the 1940s and 1950s, made a good example of what Braudel used to call the 'refusal to borrow'. Marc Bloch was regarded as an able economic historian of the Middle Ages rather than as a representative of a new style of history, while Febvre was scarcely known at all (among geographers rather than historians). When Braudel's *Mediterranean* was first published, it was not discussed in the *English Historical Review* or the *Economic History Review*. Before the 1970s, translations of books by the *Annales* historians were extremely rare. The exception to the rule was Marc Bloch. One might say that Bloch's interest in English history and his penchant for understatement (so different from the manner of Lucien Febvre) allowed him to be regarded as a sort of honorary Englishman.[10]

The reasons for the lack of translations can be found in the reviews of the major works of the school in English journals, from the *Times Literary Supplement* to the *English Historical Review*. One reviewer after another referred to what they called 'the mannered and intensely irritating Annales style', 'the quirks of style bequeathed by Lucien Febvre', or 'the esoteric jargon which sometimes suggests that the authors of the VIe Section are writing only to be understood by each other'.[11] Those of us who did support *Annales* in the early 1960s had a sense of belonging to a heretical minority, like the supporters of Bloch and Febvre in the 1930s in France.

Terms like *conjoncture* and *mentalités collectives* proved virtually impossible to translate, and extremely difficult for British historians to understand – let alone accept. Their reactions, puzzled, suspicious, or hostile, recall those of their philosopher colleagues to the work of Sartre and Merleau-Ponty. The British found, neither for the first nor the last time, that they simply did not speak the same language as the French. The difference between the British tradition of empiricism and methodological individualism and the French tradition of theory and holism inhibited intellectual contact. In England, since the days of Herbert Spencer or earlier, it was generally assumed that collective entities like 'society' are fictitious, while individuals exist.[12] Durkheim's celebrated affirmations of the reality of the social were written to demolish the assumptions of Spencer and his school. Another dramatic example of this Anglo-French debate dates from the 1920s, when the Cambridge psychologist Frederick Bartlett criticized the famous study of the social framework of memory by Maurice Halbwachs for creating a fictitious entity, 'collective memory'.[13] Today, one can still hear British historians criticizing the history of *mentalités collectives* on similar grounds.

It would be easy to multiply examples of regional variation in the reception of the new history. Even the relation between *Annales* and Marxism varied from place to place. In France, sympathy with Marxism generally went with a certain detachment from *Annales*, despite the dual loyalties of Labrousse, Vilar, Agulhon, and Vovelle. In England, by contrast, the Marxists – notably Eric Hobsbawm and Rodney Hilton – were among the first to welcome *Annales*.[14] One might explain this welcome in terms of intellectual strategy – *Annales* was an ally in the struggle against the dominance of traditional political history. It is also likely that the Marxists were impressed by the affinity between their kind of history and the French – not only the emphasis on structures and the long term but also the concern for totality (which was Marx's ideal before it was Braudel's). The affinity made them more receptive to the message of *Annales*. In Poland, the institutionalization of a form of Marxism meant that its relation with *Annales* followed yet another pattern.[15]

Annales and Other Areas of History   Another aspect of the reception of *Annales* is the spread of concepts, approaches and methods from one historical period or region to another. The movement has been dominated by students of early modern Europe (Febvre, Braudel, Le Roy Ladurie), followed closely by medievalists (Bloch, Duby, Le Goff).

There has been much less work of this kind on the nineteenth century, as we have seen, while in the case of contemporary history, it has been argued with force that *Annales* has had no impact at all. This is no accident: the importance of politics in the history of the twentieth century makes the *Annales* paradigm inapplicable to this period unless it is modified. The paradoxical conclusion reached by a sympathetic Dutch observer is that an *Annales*-style history of our own century is both necessary and impossible. 'If it is written, it will not be *Annales* history. But contemporary history can no longer be written without the *Annales*'.[16]

At the other end of the chronological spectrum, the similarity between some recent work in ancient history and the *Annales* paradigm is obvious. Whether this similarity is a case of 'impact' or affinity is rather more difficult to determine. A Durkheimian tradition in classical studies existed long before the foundation of *Annales*, a tradition exemplified by Bloch's friend Gernet in France and in England by a group of Cambridge classicists such as Jane Harrison and F. M. Cornford, who read Durkheim and Lévy-Bruhl and looked for traces of 'primitive mentality' among the ancient Greeks. In the Strasbourg era, as we have seen, a historian of Rome, André Piganiol, formed part of the *Annales* group.

Today, leading ancient historians such as Jean-Pierre Vernant and Paul Veyne draw on psychology, sociology and anthropology in order to interpret the history of Greece and Rome in a manner that runs parallel to Febvre and Braudel if it does not exactly follow their example. Vernant, for example, concerns himself with the history of categories such as space, time, and the person.[17] Veyne has written about the Roman games, drawing on the theories of Mauss and Polanyi, Veblen and Weber and analysing the financing of the games in terms of the gift, redistribution, conspicuous consumption and political corruption.[18]

Generally speaking, the history of the world outside Europe has remained relatively isolated from *Annales*. Historians of Africa, for example, have so far shown relatively little interest in this approach, apart from the Belgian anthropologist Jan Vansina, who has made the Braudelian distinction between the long, medium and short term the framework for his history of the Kuba.[19] Although a former pupil of Bloch's, Henri Brunschwig, became one of the foremost historians of colonial Africa, his study of French imperialism appears to owe little to *Annales*, doubtless because his concern with the recent past and the relatively short term (1871–1914) appeared to make this model irrelevant.[20]

The cases of Asia and America are rather more complicated. Although there are signs of increasing interest in this approach, and four members of the group were invited to a conference on 'the new history' held in New Delhi in 1988, Indian historians of India have so far taken little from *Annales*.[21] The most innovative group of Indian historians, who sail under the flag of 'subaltern studies', is well aware of the French tradition, but prefers an open Marxism. Again, despite Bloch's interest in Japan, and the general Japanese enthusiasm for Western intellectual trends, it is not easy to point to a study of Japanese history in the *Annales* tradition. A number of Japanese historians have studied at the Hautes Etudes, but they all work on the history of Europe.

Historians of other parts of Asia are a little closer to *Annales*. A recent study of south-east Asia by an Australian historian attempts a 'total history' of the region from 1450 to 1680 and takes as a model Braudel's work on material culture and everyday life.[22] Some French historians of China are also close in spirit to *Annales*. The conspicuous otherness of Chinese thought is a challenge to the history of mentalities which has provoked more than one response. One of Marc Bloch's fellow-students, the sinologist Marcel Granet, shared his enthusiasm for Durkheim and produced a major study of the Chinese world-view along Durkheimian lines, emphasizing what he called 'pre-logical thought' and the projection of the social order on to the natural world.[23]

More recently, Jacques Gernet, like other French historians of his generation, has climbed the ladder from the cellar to the attic, from the economic aspects of Buddhism to the study of Christian missions to China. His recent study of the Christian mission to China in the sixteenth and seventeenth centuries might reasonably be described as a history of mentalities in the style of *Annales*.[24] It centres on misunderstandings. The missionaries believed they had made many converts, and they failed to understand what adhesion to the new religion meant to the converts themselves. The mandarins for their part misunderstood the intentions of the missionaries.

According to Gernet, these misunderstandings reveal the differences between the categories, the 'modes of thought' (*modes de pensée*) and the 'mental framework' (*cadres mentaux*) of the two sides, associated with differences in their languages.[25] This focus on the encounter between two cultures allows Gernet to illuminate mentalities in ways denied to historians of Europe. What Braudel would have described from outside as a case of 'refusal to borrow', is interpreted by Gernet from within.

In the case of American responses to *Annales*, the contrast between north and south is extremely striking. Historians of North America – as opposed to North American historians of Europe – have so far taken little interest in the *Annales* paradigm. The anthropological turn in the history of the colonial period has developed independently of the French model. Although Braudel's work has been described as 'fascinatingly similar in its scope' to Frederick Jackson Turner's *The United States, 1830–1850*, we are still waiting for a new American Braudel.[26]

In Central and South America, the story is rather different. In Brazil, Braudel's lectures at the University of São Paulo in the

1930s are still remembered. The famous trilogy on the social history of Brazil by the historian–sociologist Gilberto Freyre (who
knew Braudel at this time) deals with topics such as the family,
sexuality, childhood, and material culture, anticipating the new
history of the 1970s and 1980s. Freyre's image of the great house
(*casa grande*) as microcosm and as metaphor of plantation society
impressed Braudel and is quoted in his work.

Again, as a series of recent studies indicates, some historians
of the Spanish and Portuguese empires in America take the
Annales paradigm very seriously indeed.[27] A good example is
Nathan Wachtel's *The Vision of the Vanquished* (1971), a history of
the early years of colonial Peru from the point of view of the
Indians. In several respects this study resembles work on Europe
by *Annales* historians. It deals in turn with economic, social, cultural, and political history. It is obviously an example of history
from below, with much to say about popular revolt. It employs
the regressive method associated with Marc Bloch, studying contemporary dances representing the Spanish conquest as a means
of recovering the Indians' original reactions. It borrows concepts
from social anthropology, notably 'acculturation', a term that
was put into circulation in France by the *Annales* historian
Alphonse Dupront. However, Wachtel does not simply take
over the *structure–conjoncture–*events model of the historians of
early modern Europe. In Peru, the socio-cultural changes of the
time did not take place within the old structures. On the contrary, the process was one of 'destructuration'. The author's concern with this process gives Wachtel's book a dynamic, and also
a tragic quality which even *The Peasants of Languedoc* cannot
match.

***Annales* and Other Disciplines**   The reception of *Annales* has
never been confined to departments of history. A movement that
drew on so many of the 'sciences of man' has naturally attracted
interest within those disciplines. Although it is more difficult
to chart the influence of less theoretical subjects like history
on more theoretical subjects like sociology than the other way
round, the attempt may be worth making.

In the intellectual development of Michel Foucault, for example, French 'new history' played a significant part. Foucault moved on parallel lines to the third generation of *Annales*. Like that generation, he was concerned to widen the subject-matter of history. He had something to teach them, as we have seen (above, p. 88). He also learned something from them.

Foucault's debt to *Annales* may well be less than what he owed to Nietzsche or to historians of science such as Georges Canguilhem (who introduced him to the notion of intellectual discontinuity), but it remains more substantial than he ever admitted. What Foucault liked to call his 'archaeology' or his 'genealogy' has at least a family resemblance to the history of mentalities. Both approaches show great concern for trends over the long term and relatively little lack of concern for individual thinkers.

What Foucault could not accept in the *Annales* approach to intellectual history was what he considered the over-emphasis on continuity.[28] It was precisely in his willingness to grasp the nettle and to discuss how world-views change that Foucault differed most from the historians of mentalities. They still have something important to learn from his emphasis on epistemological 'ruptures', however irritated they may be by his refusal to explain these discontinuities.

By the 1970s, if not before, it was possible to find archaeologists and economists reading Braudel on 'material culture', paediatricians discussing the views of Philippe Ariès on the history of childhood, and Scandinavian specialists in folklore debating with Le Roy Ladurie about folktales. Some art historians and literary critics, in the United States in particular, also cite the *Annales* historians in their own work, which they see as part of a common enterprise, sometimes described as a 'literary anthropology' or an anthropology of 'visual culture'.

In three disciplines in particular there is considerable interest in the *Annales* approach. These three disciplines are geography, sociology, and anthropology. In each case it will be noticed that in the English-speaking world at least, this interest developed relatively recently, and that it is still virtually confined to the work of Braudel.

Geography makes an appropriate place to start this survey, because there was a time when even in France geographers took the new movement more seriously than the majority of historians.[29] The affinities between the historical geography of Vidal de la Blache and the geo-history of Braudel have been discussed already and they are obvious enough. One result of the rise of Braudel's empire, however, was the decline of historical geography as a discipline in the face of competition from historians (a similar point might perhaps be made about historical sociology and historical anthropology in France).[30]

Elsewhere, the story is more complicated. Although Febvre's essay on historical geography was translated into English soon after its publication, the English-speaking world was dominated by a traditional style of geography which had little place for the French approach. This consensus broke down relatively recently, and has been replaced by pluralism, or rather by vigorous debate between supporters of the Marxist, quantitative, phenomenological and other approaches, among them that of Braudel.[31] It is worth adding that a three-volume history of the Pacific has recently been published, written not by a historian but by a geographer, Oskar Spate.[32]

In the case of sociology, the Durkheimian inspiration of the early *Annales* helped ensure it a warm reception from the first, at least in France. Two leading French sociologists, Maurice Halbwachs and Georges Friedmann, have been formally associated with the journal, while a third, Georges Gurvitch, enjoyed a collaboration with Braudel which did not exclude debate.[33] In the English-speaking world, on the other hand, it was only recently, at a time of a widespread sense of a 'crisis of sociology' that workers in the discipline rediscovered history and in the process discovered *Annales*, more particularly Braudel, whose ideas about time have obvious relevance for theorists of social change. As in the case of the historians, Marxist sociologists such as Norman Birnbaum and Immanuel Wallerstein (director of the

Fernand Braudel Center at Binghamton) were among the first to draw attention to *Annales*, but interest is now much more widespread. For example, the late Philip Abrams described Braudel's *Mediterranean* as pointing the way to 'an effective analytical historical sociology'.[34]

A few anthropologists took an early interest in *Annales*, notably Lévi-Strauss and Evans-Pritchard. Braudel and Lévi-Strauss were colleagues at the University of São Paulo in the 1930s, and continued their dialogue thereafter.[35] Evans-Pritchard, who was trained as a historian before turning anthropologist, was well aware of the work of Lucien Febvre and Marc Bloch.[36] I suspect that his famous study of *Witchcraft, Oracles and Magic* among the Azande of Central Africa owes at least some of its inspiration to Bloch's *Royal Touch*, while his analysis of the task-oriented sense of time of the Nuer of the Sudan comes to conclusions similar to those of Febvre's (formulated at much the same time) on time reckoning in the age of Rabelais.[37]

Evans-Pritchard advocated a close relation between anthropology and history at a time when most of his colleagues were ahistorical functionalists. Some younger anthropologists turned to history in the late 1960s, at much the same time as some of the *Annales* historians discovered symbolic anthropology. The two disciplines appeared to converge. However, the anthropological turn towards history was associated with a turn towards narrative and towards events, the very aspects of historical tradition that the *Annales* group had rejected. There was a danger that the two disciplines would fail to meet.

A single example will show more clearly than a list of names the conditions under which the meeting is taking place, what anthropologists want from history, or from *Annales*, and finally how a model may be transformed in the course of its application. Among the inspirations of Marshall Sahlins's historical anthropology of Hawaii is the work of Braudel, especially the essay on the *longue durée*. Braudel would doubtless have appreciated Sahlins's discussion of 'structures of the long run', in which Captain Cook's visit to Hawaii in 1779, when he was viewed by Hawaiians as a personification of their god Lono, is analysed as an example of the way in which 'events are ordered by culture'. But Sahlins does not stop there. He goes on to discuss 'how, in that process, the culture is re-ordered'.[38] Having appropriated an idea from Braudel, he subverts it, or at least transforms it, arguing that an event, Cook's visit, or more generally the encounter between Hawaiians and Europeans, led to structural changes in Hawaiian culture, such as the crisis of the taboo system, even if 'the structure was preserved in an inversion of its values'. It would be difficult to deny the potential relevance of this revised model to a discussion of, say, the socio-cultural consequences of the French Revolution. The ball is now back in the historians' court.

II STRIKING A BALANCE

It is time to sum up and attempt to assess the achievements of the *Annales* historians over three generations, discussing two questions in particular. How new, and how valuable, is their new history?

As we have seen (p. 6), the revolt of Febvre and Bloch against the dominance of the history of political events was only one of a series of such rebellions. Their principal aim, the construction of a new kind of history, has been shared by many scholars over a long period. The French tradition, from Michelet and Fustel de Coulanges to the *Année Sociologique*, Vidal de la Blache and Henri Berr, is well known. On the other hand, the alternative traditions are generally underestimated. If a fortune-teller had predicted in 1920 that a new style of history would soon develop somewhere in Europe, the obvious location for it would have been Germany, not France: the Germany of Friedrich Ratzel, Karl Lamprecht, and Max Weber.

Virtually all the innovations associated with Febvre, Bloch, Braudel, and Labrousse had precedents or parallels, from the regressive and comparative methods to the concern for interdisciplinary collaboration, for quantitative methods, and for change over the long term. In the 1930s, for example, Ernest

Labrousse and the German historian Walter Abel were working independently on the quantitative history of agricultural cycles, trends, and crises.[39] In the 1950s, the revival of regional history in France has a parallel in the revival of local history in England, associated with the school of W. G Hoskins, a disciple of Tawney whose books included a study of the making of the English landscape and an economic and social history of a single Leicestershire village, Wigston Magna, over the long term, about 900 years.[40] The French historians' enthusiasm for quantitative methods and their turn away from these methods towards microhistory and anthropology were also in step with movements in the United States and elsewhere.

If the individual innovations associated with *Annales* have precedents and parallels, the combination does not. It is also true that parallel movements for the reform and renewal of history were largely unsuccessful, from Karl Lamprecht in Germany to the 'new history' of J. H. Robinson in the United States. The achievement of Bloch, Febvre, Braudel, and their followers has been to go further than any other scholar or group of scholars in achieving these shared aims, to lead a movement that has spread more widely and lasted longer than its competitors. It may well be that the historian of the future will be able to offer explanations of this success in terms of both *structure* and *conjoncture*, looking for example at the willingness of successive French governments to fund historical research, or at the elimination of German intellectual competition in the course of two world wars.[41] The individual contribution of Bloch, Febvre and Braudel remains difficult to dismiss.

Although this book is devoted to some new trends in historical writing, I would not want to assume that innovation is necessarily desirable for its own sake. I would agree heartily with a recent critic that 'the new history is not necessarily admirable simply because it is new, nor the old contemptible simply because it is old'.[42] It is time to consider, in conclusion, the value, the cost, and the significance of the collective achievement of *Annales*.

To do this is rather like writing an obituary. In fact, the image is not altogether inappropriate. Although the Hautes Etudes still stands and still contains gifted historians who identify with the *Annales* tradition, it may not be too much to say that the movement is effectively over. On one side, we find members of the *Annales* group rediscovering politics and also the event. On the other, we see so many outsiders inspired by the movement – or moving in a similar direction for their own reasons – that terms like 'school' and even 'paradigm' are losing their meaning. The movement is dissolving, in part as a result of its success.

This movement may not have been 'all things to all people', but it has certainly been interpreted in very different ways. Traditional historians have tended to interpret its aim as the complete replacement of one kind of history by another, relegating political history and especially the history of political events to the scrapheap. I am far from sure that this was the intention of Febvre or Bloch. Innovators are usually fired by the belief that something that has not been tried before is worth doing, rather than by the determination to impose it on everyone else. In any case, political history could very well defend itself in their generation. After their time, the situation changed. Braudel claimed to be a pluralist, and liked to say that history had 'a hundred faces', but it was under his regime that the research money went to the new history at the expense of the old. It was the turn of the political historians to be marginalized.

If we are going to look at *Annales* in a global perspective, however, it makes better sense to assess it as a paradigm (or perhaps a cluster of paradigms) rather than as *the* paradigm for historical writing. It may be useful to examine the uses and the limitations of this paradigm in different fields of history, defined geographically, chronologically, and thematically. The *Annales* contribution may well be profound, but it is also extremely uneven.

As we have seen, the *Annales* group has given France the lion's share of its attention. In the wake of Braudel, a substantial number of studies have been made of the Mediterranean world, especially Spain and Italy.[43] The contribution of the *Annales* group to the history of Spanish and Portuguese America has also been a significant one. Only a small number of *Annales* historians have written about other parts of the world. Marc Bloch's interest in English history, for example, has not been pursued by his successors.

Just as they have concentrated on France, the *Annales* historians have focused their attention on one period, the so-called 'early modern' age from 1500 to 1800, more especially the 'old regime' in France from 1600 or thereabouts to 1789. Their contribution to medieval studies has also been outstanding. As we have seen, some ancient historians may be described as fellow-travellers with *Annales*.

On the other hand, the *Annales* group have paid remarkably little attention to the world since 1789. Charles Morazé, Maurice Agulhon, and Marc Ferro have done what they could to fill the gap, but it still yawns wide. The distinctive approach to history of the group, notably the lack of importance accorded to individuals and events, is surely connected with this concentration on the medieval and early modern periods. Braudel did not find it difficult to dismiss Philip II, but Napoleon, Bismarck or Stalin would have provided him with more of a challenge.

In the case of a group that sails under the flag of 'total history', it is somewhat paradoxical to examine their contributions to what is conventionally categorized as economic, social, political, and cultural history. One of the achievements of the group has been to subvert traditional categories and offer new ones, from Bloch's 'rural history' in the 1930s and Braudel's *'civilisation matérielle'* of the 1960s to the socio-cultural history of today. All the same, the importance of the contribution to economic history made by Labrousse and his followers is undeniable. It is also difficult to dispute that politics was undervalued, at least for a time (in the 1950s and 1960s), and at least by some members of the group.

Another way of assessing the *Annales* movement is to examine its leading ideas. According to a common stereotype of the group, they concern themselves with the history of structures over the long term, employ quantitative methods, claim to be scientific, and deny human freedom. Even as a description of the work of Braudel and Labrousse, this view is too simple, and it is still less adequate as a characterization of a movement that has gone through various phases and included a number of strong intellectual personalities. It may be more useful to discuss intellectual tensions within the movement. These tensions may well have been creative. Whether this is the case or not, they remain unresolved.

The conflict between freedom and determinism, or between social structure and human agency, has always divided the *Annales* historians. What distinguished Bloch and Febvre from the Marxists of their day was precisely the fact that their enthusiasm for social and economic history was not combined with the belief that economic and social forces determined everything else. Febvre was an extreme voluntarist, Bloch a more moderate one. In the second generation, on the other hand, there was a swing towards determinism, geographical in the case of Braudel and economic in that of Labrousse. Both men have been accused of taking the people out of history, and concentrating their attention on geographical structures or economic trends. In the third generation, among historians concerned with topics as diverse as matrimonial strategies or reading habits, there has been a swing back towards voluntarism. Historians of mentalities no longer assume (as Braudel did) that individuals are prisoners of their world-view, but concentrate their attention on 'resistance' to social pressures.[44]

The tension between Durkheimian sociology and the human geography of Vidal de la Blache goes back so far that it might be considered part of the structure of *Annales*. The Durkheimian tradition encouraged generalization and comparison, while the Vidalian approach concentrated on what was unique to a particular region. The founders tried to combine the two approaches, but their emphasis was different. Bloch was closer to Durkheim, Febvre (despite his concern for problem-oriented history) to Vidal. In the middle phase of the movement it was Vidal who prevailed, as the regional monographs published in the 1960s and 1970s testify. Braudel did not neglect either comparison or sociology, but he too was closer to Vidal than to Durkheim. One reason for the appeal of social anthropology to the third generation of *Annales* may be that this discipline (which faces both ways, towards the general and the particular) may help historians to find their balance.

To sum up. So far as the first generation is concerned, Braudel's assessment is worth remembering. 'Individually, neither Bloch nor Febvre was the greatest French historian of the time, but together both of them were.'[45] In the second generation, it is difficult to think of a historian of the mid-twentieth century in the class of Braudel himself. Today, a good deal of the most interesting historical work is still being done in Paris.

Looking at the movement as a whole, one sees a whole shelf of remarkable books to which it is difficult to deny the title of masterpieces: *The Royal Touch, Feudal Society, The Problem of Unbelief, The Mediterranean, The Peasants of Languedoc, Civilization and Capitalism*. It is also worth remembering the research teams that have been able to carry out enterprises demanding too much time for any individual to bring any one of them to a successful conclusion. The long life of the movement has allowed historians to build on one another's work (as well as to react against some of it). To name only the most important developments in *Annales* history is to make an impressive list: problem-oriented history, comparative history, historical psychology, geo-history, the history of the long term, serial history, historical anthropology.

In my own view, the outstanding achievement of the *Annales* group, over all three generations, has been the reclaiming of vast areas for history. The group has extended the territory of the historian to unexpected areas of human behaviour and to social groups neglected by traditional historians. These extensions of historical territory are associated with the discovery of new sources and the development of new methods to exploit them. They are also associated with collaboration with other disciplines that study humanity, from geography to linguistics, and from economics to psychology. This interdisciplinary collaboration has been sustained over more than sixty years, a phenomenon without parallel in the history of the social sciences.

It is for these reasons that the title of this book refers to the 'French Historical Revolution', and that the Introduction began with the words, 'A remarkable amount of the most innovative, the most memorable and the most significant historical writing of the twentieth century has been produced in France.' The discipline will never be the same again.

Glossary: The Language of *Annales*

This brief glossary is intended primarily as a guide to readers who are not accustomed to the language of the *Annales* historians. The historical notes are as accurate as I can make them, but they will doubtless be corrected by philologists in due course.

civilization the most difficult term to define in the *Annales* trinity. Before it appeared in the title of the journal in 1946, it had been employed by Bloch in his *French Rural History*. It was also a favourite term of the anthropologist Marcel Mauss, and, following him, of Braudel. In all these cases it might be best to translate the term into 'culture' in the broad anthropological sense. Thus Braudel's *civilisation matérielle* can be rendered 'material culture'.

conjoncture in the language of French economists, this term is the normal word for 'trend'. (It had earlier been used by German economists such as Ernst Wagemann in his *Konjunkturlehre* of 1928, and historians such as Wilhelm Abel in his 1935 study of *Agrarkonjunktur*.) Braudel helped to put it into historical circulation by speaking of *la conjoncture générale du XVIe siècle* in his inaugural lecture of 1950. At this point the word implied (as one might expect from its etymology, *coniungere*, to conjoin) a sense of connection between diverse but simultaneous phenomena.

When it was generally adopted by the *Annales* historians, however, the term was often used as the complementary opposite to *structure*, to refer is other words to the short- or medium- rather than to the long-term, without the implication of lateral connections (Chaunu (1955–60), vol. 2, pp. 9–13; Burguière (1986), pp. 152–3).

ethnohistoire   a false friend. What the English-speaking world calls 'anthropology' is often described in French as *ethnologie*. Consequently, *ethnohistoire* means 'historical anthropology' (which it might be more exact to call 'anthropological history') rather than 'ethno-history' in the American sense of the history of non-literate peoples.

histoire événementielle   a dismissive term for the history of events, launched by Braudel in the preface to his *Mediterranean*, but already used by Paul Lacombe in 1915 (while the idea goes back further still, to Simiand, Durkheim and indeed to the eighteenth century).

histoire globale   an ideal formulated by Braudel. 'Globality is not the claim to write a complete history of the world [*histoire totale du monde*] . . . it is simply the desire, when one confronts a problem, to go systematically beyond its limits' (Braudel (1978), p. 245). Thus Braudel himself studied his Mediterranean sea in the context of a 'greater Mediterranean', from the Sahara to the Atlantic. The term seems to have been borrowed from the sociology of Georges Gurvitch. Cf. **histoire totale**.

histoire de l'imaginaire   a recent term, employed for example by Duby (1978) and Corbin (1982), which more or less corresponds to the old *histoire des représentations collectives*. The old term had Durkheimian associations, while the 'imaginary' has neo-Marxist ones. It seems to have been taken from C. Castoriadis, *L'institution imaginaire de la société* (1975), a study that is in turn in debt to Althusser's celebrated definition of ideology in terms of an 'imagined relationship to real conditions of existence'.

histoire immobile   sometimes translated 'motionless history' or 'history that stands still', a phrase used in 1973 by Le Roy Ladurie in a lecture about the eco-system of early modern France, which was attacked as if he had denied the existence of change in history (Le Roy Ladurie (1978a), pp. 1–27). Braudel (1949) had already written of *une histoire quasi immobile* in the preface to his *Mediterranean*.

histoire-problème   'problem-oriented history', a slogan of Lucien Febvre's, who thought all history should take this form.

histoire quantitative   another false friend, since the term often refers in French not to quantitative history in general, but to macroeconomic history, the history of the Gross National Product in the past. Some kinds of quantitative history are known in French as *histoire sérielle*. See Burguière (1986), pp. 557–62.

histoire sérielle   a term employed by Chaunu in 1960, and rapidly taken up by Braudel and others, to refer to the analysis of trends over the *longue durée* (q.v.) by means of the study of continuities and discontinuities within a series of relatively homogeneous data (wheat prices, dates of wine harvests, annual births, Easter communicants, etc.). Cf. Chaunu (1970, 1973); Burguière (1986), pp. 631–3.

histoire totale   Febvre liked to speak of *histoire tout court*, as opposed to economic or social or political history. R. H. Tawney, in 1932, used the term *histoire intégrale*, perhaps on a French model. But the anthropologist Marcel Mauss liked to use the adjective *totale* to characterize the approach of his discipline. Braudel employed the term in the conclusion to the second edition of his *Mediterranean* and elsewhere. Cf. Devulder (1985). See also **histoire globale**.

longue durée   this phrase became a technical term after its employment by Braudel in a famous article (Braudel (1958)). A similar conception underlies his *Mediterranean*, but in that book he wrote of *une histoire quasi immobile* (for the very long term) and *une historire lentement rythmée* (for changes over a mere century or two).

mentalité although Durkheim and Mauss had employed it on occasion, it was Lévy-Bruhl's *La mentalité primitive* (1922) that launched this term in France. All the same, despite his reading of Lévy-Bruhl, Marc Bloch preferred to describe his *Royal Touch* (1924), now recognized as a pioneering work in the history of mentalities, as a history of *représentations collectives* (a term favoured by Durkheim), *représentations mentales,* or even *illusions collectives*. In the 1930s, Febvre introduced the term *outillage mental,* but it did not have great success. It was Georges Lefebvre, a historian on the edge of the *Annales* group, who launched the phrase *histoire des mentalités collectives*.

nouvelle histoire the term was popularized by the book *La nouvelle histoire* (1978), edited by Jacques Le Goff and others, but this claim for *Annales* had been made earlier. Braudel had spoken of *une histoire nouvelle* in his inaugural lecture at the Collège de France (1950). Febvre had used phrases like 'another kind of history' (*une autre histoire*) to describe what the *Annales* group were trying to do.

outillage mental see **mentalité**.

psychologie historique the term was used by Henri Berr in 1900 when formulating the aim of his newly founded *Revue de Synthèse Historique*. Bloch described his *Royal Touch* (1924) as a contribution to *la psychologie religieuse,* and some of his later essays on responses to technological change as contributions to *la psychologie collective*. Febvre pleaded for *la psychologie historique* in an article of 1938, published in the *Encyclopédie française,* and he described his study of Rabelais (1942) in the same terms. Robert Mandrou subtitled his *Introduction à la France moderne* (1961), based on the notes left by Febvre, and published in a series founded by Berr, '*essai de psychologie historique*'. More recently, in the competition with 'mentalities', this term has been the loser.

structure Febvre employed the term 'structure' on occasion, but he was also somewhat suspicious of it. Braudel made little use of the word in his *Mediterranean,* in which what we might call the structural sections are described as '*le part du milieu*' and '*destins collectifs*'. It seems to have been Chaunu who launched the term, which he defined as 'everything in a society or an economy which lasts sufficiently long for its movement to escape the ordinary observer' (Chaunu (1955–60), vol. 1, p. 12; cf. Burguière (1986), pp. 644–6).

Notes

INTRODUCTION

1   Le Goff et al. (1978).
2   The journal has had four titles: *Annales d'histoire économique et sociale* (1929–39); *Annales d'histoire sociale* (1939–42, 1945); *Mélanges d'histoire sociale* (1942–4); *Annales: économies, sociétés, civilisations* (1946–).
3   At an international discussion of the *Annales* school at Stuttgart in 1985, Marc Ferro vigorously denied the existence of the school. While so doing, he constantly employed the term 'nous'.
4   Febvre (1953), p. 32.
5   Febvre (1953), pp. 104–6, a letter written in 1933.
6   Braudel (1949) (English trans., 1975 edn), vol. 1, p. 22.
7   Or perhaps, like R. Chartier and J. Revel, of '*une sorte de nébuleuse en expansion constante et dotée d'une capacité d'attraction et d'amalgame remarquable*' (quoted in Coutau-Bégarie (1983), p. 259).
8   On Bloch's drafts, see Mastrogregori (1989). On other Bloch manuscripts, see Fink (1989).
9   What he calls the 'strategy' of *Annales* is analysed in a rather crude, reductionist manner by Coutau-Bégarie (1983). It is studied with more finesse by Burguière (1979). For an example of Febvre as a politician, see Charle and Delangle (1987).
10 On the journal, see Wesseling and Oosterhoff (1986).
11 'Pour une histoire dirigée', reprinted in Febvre (1953), pp. 55–60.

1 THE OLD HISTORIOGRAPHICAL REGIME AND ITS CRITICS

1 Further details and references in Burke (1988).
2 On this process, see Gilbert (1965) and Boer (1987).
3 Michelet (1842), p. 8.
4 Coleman (1987), pp. 38ff.
5 Hauser (1899); Sée (1901); Mantoux (1906).
6 As Himmelfarb (1987), p. 152, points out, Green's text belies some of these claims.
7 Comte (1864), leçon 52, pp. 10ff.
8 Spencer (1861), pp. 26ff.
9 Durkheim (1896), p. v.
10 Cf. Iggers (1975), pp. 27ff, on what he calls 'The Crisis of the Conventional Conception of "Scientific" History'.
11 Lamprecht (1894), foreword; Lamprecht (1904). On him, see Weintraub (1966), ch. 4.
12 Robinson (1912). On him, see Hendricks (1946).
13 Lavisse (1900–12). The geographer was Paul Vidal de la Blache, and the cultural historian was Henri Lemonnier. On Lavisse, see Boer (1987), pp. 205ff.
14 Simiand (1903).
15 Langlois and Seignebos (1897). On him, see Boer (1987), pp. 218ff.
16 Siegel (1983).
17 Erikson (1954).

2 THE FOUNDERS: LUCIEN FEBVRE AND MARC BLOCH

1 On Febvre as *combatif et véhément*, see Braudel (1953a), p. 15.
2 Some disagreements are noted in Fink (1989), pp. 185, 200, 261.
3 Lukes (1973), p. 45.
4 Peyrefitte (1946).
5 On Febvre and Bergson, see Braudel (1972), p. 465.
6 On Vidal, see Buttimer (1971), pp. 43ff.
7 *Revue de Synthèse Historique*, 12 (1906), 249–61; 23 (1911), 131–47; 27 (1913), 52–65; 38 (1924), 37–53; 42 (1926), 19–40.
8 Febvre (1953), p. vi. Cf. Venturi (1966), pp. 5–70.
9 Febvre (1911), p. 323.
10 Jaurès (1901), pp. 65ff.

11 On Ratzel, see Buttimer (1971), pp. 27ff.
12 Febvre (1922), p. 284.
13 Febvre (1922), pp. 402ff.
14 Lukes (1973), pp. 58ff.
15 Cf. Bloch in *Annales* (1935), p. 393: '*A la vieille année les historiens de ma génération ont du plus qu'ils ne sauraient dire.*'
16 Bloch (1913), p. 122.
17 Bloch (1913), pp. 60–1.
18 For reminiscences of Strasbourg at that time, see Baulig (1957–8), and Dollinger in Carbonell and Livet (1983), pp. 65ff. Having taught at a new university in its first years of activity (at Sussex in the early 1960s), I can testify to the intellectual excitement and the stimulus to innovation to be found in such an environment.
19 Febvre (1945), p. 391.
20 Febvre (1953), p. 393.
21 On Blondel, see Febvre (1953), pp. 370–5. Halbwachs (1925), discussed by Bloch in *Revue de Synthèse Historique*, 40 (1925), 73–83.
22 Febvre (1953) cites Bremond on six occasions.
23 Lefebvre (1932); Bloch, *Revue de Synthèse Historique* (1921).
24 Piganiol (1923), especially pp. 103ff, 141ff. On him, F. Hartog in Carbonell and Livet (1983), pp. 41ff.
25 Good discussions in Ginzburg (1965) and Le Goff (1983).
26 Bloch (1924), p. 18.
27 Bloch (1924), pp. 21, 51.
28 Bloch (1924), pp. 21, 360ff.
29 Bloch (1924), pp. 420ff.
30 Bloch (1924), p. 429.
31 Popper (1935), pp. 40ff.
32 Bloch (1924), p. vi.
33 Bloch (1924), p. 421n.
34 Bloch (1924), pp. 21, 51, 409.
35 Febvre (1945), 392; cf. Rhodes (1978).
36 Bloch (1924), pp. 52ff, 421n.
37 Bloch (1928).
38 Febvre (1953) confesses that this interest of his was encouraged by reading Stendhal's books on Italy.
39 Febvre (1962), pp. 529–603, especially pp. 573, 581.
40 Febvre (1929), reprinted in Febvre (1957), p. 38, trans. Febvre (1973), p. 66. Febvre's phrasing, incidentally, recalls the title of the famous study by Henri Bremond, whose importance for Febvre has already been noted (see p. 16 of this volume).

41 Febvre (1928), pp. 104ff, 287ff. On ways to combine the new history with biography, see Le Goff (1989).

42 Febvre (1945), pp. 398ff; Leuilliot (1973), pp. 317ff; Fink (1989), ch. 7.

43 *'Nous entendons créer une revue qui puisse exercer dans le domaine des études d'histoire économique et sociale, le rôle de direction'* (Febvre (1928), q Leuilliot (1973), p. 319).

44 *Annales*, 1, p. 1. Cf. Febvre's letters of the time on *'la nécessité primordiale d'abattre les cloisons'* and the function of the journal *'comme agent de liaison entre géographes, économistes, historiens, sociologues, etc'* (Leuilliot, (1973), p. 321).

45 Pomian (1986), p. 385, suggests that the roles of Pirenne, Rist and Siegfried were largely honorific.

46 *Annales*, 2, p. 2. Cf. a letter by Bloch quoted by Leuilliot (1973), p. 318, *'nous tenons au mot social'*.

47 All reprinted in Bloch (1967).

48 Bloch (1948).

49 L. Febvre, 'Avertissement au lecteur', prefixed to the Paris, 1952 edn of Bloch (1931).

50 Bloch (1931), pp. xi, 64.

51 Bloch (1931), p. xii.

52 Bloch (1925, p. 81) remarked *'combien il est regrettable que l'oeuvre de ce grand esprit que fut F. W. Maitland soit trop peu lue en France'*.

53 Fustel (1864), Book 2, ch. 10. The references to Maitland, Seebohm and Fustel in Bloch (1931), pp. xi–xii, minimize the parallels to his regressive method. But Bloch (1949) pays tribute to Maitland in this respect.

54 Bloch (1939–40), pp. 363, 368, 379.

55 Ibid., p. 156.

56 Febvre (1953), pp. 3–43, 55–60, 207–38, etc.

57 'Leur histoire et la nôtre' (1938), reprinted in Febvre (1953), pp. 276–83; 'Sur une forme d'histoire qui n'est pas la nôtre' (1947), reprinted in Febvre (1953), pp. 114–18. Cf. Cobb (1966).

58 *Annales* (1939), p. 5.

59 Duby (1987); Duby and Lardreau (1980), p. 40.

60 Febvre (1953), pp. 427–8, hints as much in his review of Bloch's book.

61 Bloch (1949), ch. 1.

62 The anti-Semitic policies of the Vichy regime required the removal of Bloch from the co-direction of *Annales*. Bloch thought the

journal should cease publication, but Febvre overruled him. Cf. N. Z. Davis (1989) 'Censorship, Silence and Resistance, the *Annales* during the German Occupation of France', unpublished paper for Moscow conference on *Annales*, October 1989.

63 Wootton (1988).
64 Among the most perceptive criticisms of the book is Frappier (1969).
65 Febvre and Martin (1958).
66 Mandrou (1961).
67 Febvre (1953), p. 16.
68 Ecclesiastical images come naturally to mind when writing about Febvre, from 'the combative prelate' (Raulff, 1988) to 'the Febvre pontificate' (Hughes, 1969).

3   THE AGE OF BRAUDEL

1 Braudel (1928).
2 Braudel (1972).
3 Braudel (1953a), esp. p. 5; cf. Febvre (1953), p. 432.
4 Braudel (1972).
5 Braudel (1949: 1975 edn), p. 1017.
6 Ibid., pp. 372, 966.
7 Ibid., p. 1101.
8 Ibid., p. 1104.
9 Braudel (1980), p. 10.
10 Ibid., p. 21.
11 Ibid., p. 363.
12 Ibid., pp. 660–1.
13 Ibid., pp. 704ff. The term 'treason' alludes to the famous essay by Julien Benda, *La trahison des clercs*.
14 Ibid., pp. 757ff.
15 Ibid., p. 20.
16 Ibid., pp. 34ff.
17 Ibid., p. 137.
18 Ibid., p. 22.
19 E.g. Cvijic (1918).
20 Ratzel (1897), esp. chs 13 and 21.
21 Mauss (1930), 231–52. Cf. Braudel (1969), pp. 201–3.

22 Pirenne (1937).

23 The most important are Bailyn (1951) and Hexter (1972).

24 Guilmartin (1974), esp. pp. 234, 251. On the other hand, Hess (1972) argues that Braudel overestimated its importance.

25 Braudel (1969), p. 208.

26 Peristiany (1965); Blok (1981).

27 Hasluck (1929). In 1977 I asked Braudel his opinion of this book, but he had not heard of it.

28 Bailyn (1951).

29 *Annales* (1949), quoted in Hexter (1972), p. 105.

30 'Braudel and the Primary Vision', a conversation with P. Burke and H. G. Koenigsberger, broadcast on Radio 3, 13 November 1977.

31 The suggestion comes from Hexter (1972), p. 104, noting that Braudel (1958) virtually admits this.

32 J. H. Elliott, *New York Review of Books*, 3 May 1973.

33 Braudel (1969), p. 31. For vigorous criticism of this view, see Vovelle (1982), esp. pt 4.

34 Braudel (1949), p. 1244.

35 Braudel (1949), p. 755.

36 Braudel discussed Sorre's work in *Annales* (1943), reprinted in Braudel (1969), pp. 105–16. Cf. Dion (1934); Sereni (1961); Péguy (1986).

37 Braudel (1949), p. 170.

38 Ibid., p. 22. The phrase about his 'vast appetite' comes from Hexter (1972), p. 119.

39 Braudel (1949), p. 21; Braudel (1958).

40 Braudel (1969), p. 31, cites Curtius (1948), a book dedicated to Aby Warburg and inspired by his work.

41 Braudel (1969), pp. 26ff.

42 Dumoulin (1986).

43 Braudel wrote the introduction to the first volume of Ports – Routes – Trafics, claiming that the collection 'would represent the essential part of our work'.

44 Le Goff (1987), p. 224, denies any connection with the events of 1968.

45 Braudel (1968b), p. 349.

46 Chaunu (1987), p. 71.

47 Lapeyre (1955), dedicated to Braudel; Delumeau (1957–9); Bennassar (1967).

48 Braudel (1967: 1981 edn, p. 23) says that Febvre made his suggestion in 1952; Braudel (1977), p. 3, gives the date as 1950.

49 Braudel (1979a) is the revised version.

50 Braudel (1979a), pp. 23–6.

51 Originally translated into English under the title *Capitalism and Material Life* (London, 1973).

52 On Wagemann, Braudel (1979a), p. 34; cf. Braudel (1969), pp. 133–42.

53 Troels-Lund (1879–1901).

54 Note the positive remarks about Spengler in Braudel (1969), pp. 186ff, as well as the references to him in the index to Braudel (1979a; 1979b).

55 Braudel (1979a), ch. 4.

56 This criticism has been made in Burke (1981), pp. 38ff; and Clark (1985), pp. 191f.

57 Stone (1965).

58 See, for example, Appadurai (1986).

59 Goffman (1959). For a discussion of houses from this point of view, see Le Roy Ladurie (1975). For clothes, see Roche (1989).

60 Braudel (1979b), pp. 118, 463ff, 244ff.

61 Ibid., pp. 225ff.

62 Ibid., p. 166.

63 Ibid., pp. 402–3.

64 Braudel (1969), p. 51.

65 Wallerstein (1974–80).

66 Gunder Frank (1969), pp. 32ff.

67 Braudel (1981).

68 For an appreciation, see Aymard (1988); for severe criticisms by a geographer, see Lacoste (1988).

69 Cf. Hexter (1972), p. 113, on Braudel's 'light-hearted' use of statistics.

70 Braudel (1969), p. 186.

71 For an overview, see Le Roy Ladurie (1973), pp. 7–16.

72 Wiebe (1895).

73 Febvre (1962), pp. 190–1.

74 Simiand (1932).

75 Labrousse (1933).

76 The reference to the 'margin' comes from Allegra and Torre (1977), pp. 328ff. Labrousse (1980) expresses his identification with *Annales*.

77   Cf. Suratteau (1983).
78   Labrousse (1933, 1944). A critique of these studies is given in Landes (1950). See also Renouvin (1971), and Labrousse (1980).
79   Reprinted in Braudel (1969), pp. 25–54.
80   Chaunu (1955–60), vol. 8, pt 1, p. xiv.
81   At the International Congress of Historical Sciences at Rome in 1955, Labrousse gave an important paper, 'Voies nouvelles vers une histoire de la bourgeoisie occidentale'. He also supervised Daumard's thesis on the Paris bourgeoisie.
82   Labrousse (1980); Labrousse (1970).
83   Braudel had also collaborated with the Italian historian Ruggiero Romano in a quantitative study of shipping at the port of Leghorn (Livorno).
84   It runs to twelve volumes, mainly statistics, but volume 8, the interpretative part, includes more than 3,000 pages of text.
85   Best expressed in Chaunu (1964), pp. 11–38.
86   Henry (1956); Henry and Gautier (1958).
87   Meuvret (1946, 1977).
88   Goubert (1982).
89   Regional studies directed by Labrousse also include those of Maurice Agulhon on Provence, Pierre Deyon on Amiens, Adeline Daumard on the Paris bourgeoisie, J. Georgelin on Venice, J. Nicolas on Savoy.
90   Buttimer (1971), pp. 74ff.
91   Saint-Jacob (1960), Baehrel (1961), Frèche (1974), etc.
92   Deyon (1967), Garden (1970), Gascon (1971), Delumeau (1957–9), Bennassar (1967), etc.
93   Chaunu (1970).
94   Le Roy Ladurie (1973), p. 7.
95   Duby (1953). Cf. Duby (1987), pp. 126–7.
96   Corbin (1975).
97   It was Gaston Zeller, a professor of international relations, who inspired both Delumeau (1957–9) and Gascon (1971).
98   Arriaza (1980) argues for Mousnier's dependence on Bernard Barber. But he is well aware of other American sociologists, let alone Max Weber.
99   Mousnier (1964) is a critique of the contributions by Daumard and Furet to the Labrousse project for a quantitative analysis of the social structure. Compare Mousnier (1968b) on castes, orders and classes, with Labrousse (1973).

100   Corvisier (1964); Couturier (1969).
101   Porshnev (1948).
102   Mousnier (1968a); Pillorget (1975); Bercé (1974).
103   Le Roy Ladurie (1966), p. 11.
104   Le Roy Ladurie (1967).
105   Le Roy Ladurie (1959), p. 157.
106   Le Roy Ladurie (1966), p. 243.
107   Ibid., p. 311.
108   Some criticisms were offered by Yves Bercé in *Bibliothèque de l'école des Chartes*, 125 (1967), pp. 444–50.
109   Garrett (1985).
110   North (1978), p. 80.
111   Brenner (1976), esp. p. 31; Le Roy Ladurie (1978b).

4   THE THIRD GENERATION

1   Dosse (1987).
2   On smells, see Corbin (1982).
3   Klapisch (1985); Farge (1986); Ozouf (1976); Perrot (1974).
4   Faure (1980); Stuard (1981).
5   Vovelle (1982) admits following this itinerary, and notes that the phrase was coined by Emmanuel Le Roy Ladurie, before he moved in a similar direction.
6   Ariès (1960).
7   Among the most cogent critics are Herlihy (1978), pp. 109–31; Hunt (1970), pp. 32–51; and Pollock (1983).
8   Febvre (1973), p. 24.
9   Ariès (1977).
10   For a balanced assement of Ariès, see McManners (1981), pp. 116ff.
11   Flandrin (1976).
12   Among those who attended his seminars were Jean-Louis Flandrin, Dominique Julia, Mona Ozouf, and Daniel Roche.
13   Braudel (1969), pp. 32, 57.
14   Dupront (1961, 1965, 1974, 1987).
15   Joutard and Lecuir (1985).
16   Mandrou (1961).
17   Mandrou (1968).

18 Delumeau (1971, 1978, 1983). On the idea of a history of fear, see Febvre (1973), p. 24.
19 Le Roy Ladurie (1966), pp. 196, 284.
20 Le Roy Ladurie (1978a), ch. 3.
21 Besançon (1968) and (1971).
22 Reprinted in Le Goff (1977), pp. 29–42.
23 Febvre (1942), pp. 393–9.
24 Le Goff (1981), pp. 227ff, a phrase used as the title of a study by one of his pupils; see Chiffoleau (1980).
25 Duby (1978).
26 Althusser (1970); Duby (1987), p. 119, confesses his debt to Althusser.
27 Vovelle (1982), esp. pp. 5–17.
28 Chaunu (1973).
29 Translated in Febvre (1973), pp. 193–207.
30 Le Bras (1931).
31 Febvre reviewed this work in *Annales* in 1943 (1973, pp. 268–75).
32 Pérouas (1964). Compare the approach of Marcilhacy (1964).
33 Lebrun (1971); Vovelle (1973); Chiffoleau (1980); Croix (1983).
34 Chaunu et al. (1978). Chaunu (1987), p. 92, admits to having been '*bouleversé*' by Vovelle's thesis.
35 For a lucid and judicious survey of this body of work, see McManners (1981).
36 Fleury and Valmary (1957).
37 Furet and Ozouf (1977).
38 Roche and Chartier (1974).
39 Mandrou (1964).
40 Bollême et al. (1965).
41 Martin (1969).
42 Martin and Chartier (1983–6).
43 Roche (1981), ch. 7.
44 Roche (1989).
45 Duby (1973a).
46 On this turn, Burguière (1978).
47 Bourdieu and Passeron (1970); Chartier et al. (1976).
48 Bourdieu (1972).
49 De Certeau (1975), chs 6, 8.
50 De Certeau et al. (1975).
51 De Certeau (1980).
52 De Certeau (1975).

53 Le Goff (1977), pp. 225–87; cf. Schmitt (1984).
54 Le Roy Ladurie (1975).
55 Le Roy's models include Redfield (1930); Wylie (1957); and Pitt-Rivers (1961).
56 Originally an Italian term, referring in the first instance to Carlo Ginzburg's study (1976) – again from inquisition records – of the world-view of a sixteenth-century miller.
57 Among the most penetrating criticisms are those of Davis (1979); Boyle (1981); and Rosaldo (1986).
58 Le Roy Ladurie (1975), p. 9. The reference is to the French edition, since a new introduction was written for the abbreviated English translation.
59 In Chartier (1988) the only extended discussion of historical anthropology occurs in the course of a critique of Darnton (1984).
60 Cf. De Certeau (1975), ch. 5, on 'the space of the other'.
61 Chartier (1988), chs. 5, 7, 8.
62 Quoted by Chartier (1988), p. 61.
63 Chartier (1987) collects them into one volume.
64 Ibid., p. 257.
65 Bourdieu (1972); De Certeau (1980).
66 Nora (1986).
67 On 'le retour du politique', cf. Julliard (1974).
68 Le Roy Ladurie (1982). The group included Agulhon, Besançon, Furet, Labrousse, Le Roy Ladurie, and Vovelle.
69 Goubert (1966, 1973).
70 Bercé (1974); Pillorget (1975); Beik (1985).
71 Le Roy Ladurie (1987).
72 Le Goff (1972).
73 Agulhon (1970).
74 The impression would be stronger if the original doctoral thesis had not been published in separate parts, excluding from this volume a study of Toulon.
75 On his move towards 'l'eclecticisme et l'empirisme', see Agulhon (1987).
76 Thompson (1963), pp. 416ff.
77 Agulhon (1970), pp. 254–60. The author notes on p. 368 that his carnival is 'neither the son nor the younger brother' of the Carnival of Romans. For similar approaches to nineteenth-century France, see Corbin (1975) and Perrot (1974).
78 Agulhon (1979).

79 Nora (1986), pp. 167–93.
80 For example, Le Roy Ladurie (1975).
81 On 'le renouvellement de l'histoire politique', see Julliard (1974).
82 Le Goff (1989); Vovelle (1975); Roche (1982).
83 Stone (1979), p. 8.
84 Braudel (1949); p. 21.
85 Ricoeur (1983–5), vol. 1, pp. 289ff.
86 Duby (1973a and b).
87 Giddens (1977).
88 Bois (1960). It may be worth observing that this study begins with a favourable reference to Febvre, and makes use of the regressive method associated with Bloch.
89 Le Roy Ladurie (1973), pp. 111–32.
90 Le Roy Ladurie (1979). The phrase 'social drama' comes from the anthropologist Victor Turner, cited by Le Roy Ladurie in his book.
91 On 1917 and 1914–18, see Ferro (1967, 1969); Furet and Vovelle are among the leading historians of the French Revolution.
92 Furet and Halévi (1989), p. 4.

5   THE *ANNALES* IN GLOBAL PERSPECTIVE

1 On the '*Annales* paradigm', see Stoianovich (1976). A special issue of the journal *Review* (1978) was devoted to 'The Impact of the Annales School on the Social Sciences'. See also Gil Pujol (1983).
2 Eric Hobsbawm recalls that as a student at Cambridge in the 1930s, he went to a lecture by Marc Bloch, who was presented to the audience as the greatest living medievalist. *Review* (1978), p. 158.
3 A serious study of the circulation figures would be needed to support this generalization.
4 A general discussion of *Annales* in Italy in Aymard (1978). The first volume of the Einaudi *Storia d'Italia*, edited by Braudel's associate Romano, was called *Caratteri originali*, a reference to Bloch's *Caractères originaux de L' histoire rurale française*.
5 Malowist (1972).
6 Braudel (1958); cf. Pomian (1978).
7 Braudel (1978), p. 250. Kula (1960) comments on Braudel's essay.

8   Kula (1962).
9   Cf. Iggers (1975), pp,. 80ff, 192ff.
10 The major exceptions are Febvre (1922, 1928) and Bloch (1931, 1939–40, 1949).
11 Further details and references in Burke (1978).
12 It might be instructive to compare the terms in which English sociologists criticized Durkheim; English psychologists, Halbwachs; and English historians, *Annales*.
13 Bartlett (1932).
14 Hobsbawm (1978).
15 The special issue of *Review* (1978) includes many comments on the relation between *Annales* and Marxism.
16 Wesseling (1978).
17 Vernant (1966), It is subtitled a study of 'psychologie historique'. The author pays homage not to Febvre but to the psychologist I. Meyerson.
18 Veyne (1976).
19 Vansina (1978). See especially pp. 10, 112, 197, 235. For a debate on the relevance of the *Annales* approach to African history, see Clarence-Smith (1977) and Vansina (1978).
20 Brunschwig (1960). Some younger historians of Africa are closer to the Braudel tradition.
21 As in the case of Africa, some French historians of India owe a greater debt to the *Annales* tradition.
22 Reid (1988). Cf. Lombard (1976), a global study of a small state. The author's father, Maurice Lombard, was a distinguished medievalist associated with *Annales*.
23 Granet (1934).
24 Gernet (1982). The author is the son of the classicist Louis Gernet, and his thesis was directed by H. Demiéville, a former pupil of Labrousse.
25 Ibid., pp. 12, 189. The references are to the French edition.
26 On Turner and Braudel, see Andrews (1978), p. 173. For a more ambivalent reaction, see Henretta (1979).
27 Notably Wachtel (1971); Lafaye (1974); Mauro (1963); Murra et al. (1986); a collection of articles from *Annales*); Gruzinski (1988).
28 Foucault (1969), p. 32. Chartier (1988), p. 57, notes that Foucault was 'an attentive reader' of the serial history of the 1950s and 1960s.
29 Duby (1987), p. 133.

30 Baker (1984), p. 2.
31 Ibid.
32 Spate (1979–88).
33 Braudel (1953b).
34 Birnbaum (1978); Wallerstein (1974–80), vol. 1; Abrams (1982), pp. 333ff.
35 Most recently in Lévi-Strauss (1983).
36 Evans-Pritchard (1961), p. 48, cites Febvre and Bloch. He also cites Pirenne, Vidal, Granet, Dumézil, Meillet, and Saussure.
37 Evans-Pritchard (1937). Compare the passage on the self-confirming character of belief in the poison oracle (p. 194) with Bloch on the royal touch (above, pp. 17–18). Evans-Pritchard, who studied medieval history before turning anthropologist, had probably read Bloch.
38 Sahlins (1981), p. 8. Cf. Sahlins (1985).
39 Abel (1935), a study that was only discovered by French historians after the war.
40 Hoskins (1955, 1957).
41 Structural–conjunctural explanations are offered by Coutau-Bégarie (1983) and Wallerstein (1988).
42 Himmelfarb (1987), p. 101.
43 Aymard, Bennassar, Chaunu, Delille, Delumeau, Georgelin, Klapisch, Lapeyre.
44 Vovelle (1982).
45 Braudel (1968a), p. 93.

Bibliography

This bibliography includes:
i   every work cited in the notes;
ii   a selection of studies by members of the *Annales* group;
iii a full but not exhaustive list of studies about them.

Unless otherwise specified, the place of publication is Paris.

Abel, W. (1935) *Agrarkrisen und Agrarkonjonktur* (second edn, Hamburg and Berlin 1966).

Abrams, P. (1982) *Historical Sociology*, Newton Abbot, England.

Aguet, J.-P. and Muller, B. (1985) ' "Combats pour l'histoire" de Lucien Febvre dans le Revue de Synthèse Historique', *Revue suisse d'histoire*, 35, 389–448.

Agulhon, M. (1968) *Pénitents et francs-maçons de l'ancienne Provence*.

Agulhon, M. (1970) *La République au village* (English trans.: *The Republic in the Village*, Cambridge 1982).

Agulhon, M. (1979) *Marianne au combat* (English trans.: *Marianne into Battle*, Cambridge 1981).

Agulhon, M. (1987) 'Vu des coulisses', in Nora (1987), pp. 9–59.

Allegra, L. and Torre, A. (1977) *La nascita della storia sociale in Francia dalla Comune alle Annales*, Turin.

Althusser, L. (1970) 'Idéologie et appareils idéologiques d'état', *La Pensée* (1970) (English trans. in his *Lenin and Philosophy*, London 1971).

Andrews, R. M. (1978) 'Implications of Annales for U.S. History', *Review*, 1, 165–80.

Appadurai, A. (ed.) (1986) *The Social Life of Things*, Cambridge.

Ariès, P. (1960) *L'enfance et la vie familiale sous l'ancien régime* (English trans.: *Centuries of Childhood*, New York 1965).

Ariès, P. (1977) *L'homme devant la mort* (English trans.: *The Hour of Our Death*, London 1981).

Arriaza, A. (1980) 'Mousnier, Barber and the "Society of Orders"', *Past and Present*, 89, 39–57.

Aymard, M. (1978) 'The Impact of the Annales School in Mediterranean Countries', *Review*, 1, 53–64.

Aymard, M. (1988) 'Une certaine passion de la France' in *Lire Braudel*, pp. 58–73.

Baehrel, R. (1961) *Une croissance, la basse Provence rurale*.

Bailyn, B. (1951) 'Braudel's Geohistory – a Reconsideration', *Journal of Economic History*, 11, 277–82.

Baker, A. R. H. (1984) 'Reflections on the Relations of Historical Geography and the Annales School of History', *Explorations in Historical Geography*, ed. A. R. H. Baker and D. Gregory, Cambridge, 1–27.

Bartlett, F. C. (1932) *Remembering: A Study in Experimental and Social Psychology*.

Baulig, H. (1945) 'Marc Bloch géographe', *Annales*, 8, 5–12.

Baulig, H. (1957–8) 'Lucien Febvre à Strasbourg', *Bull. Fac. Lettres Strasbourg*, 36, 185–8.

Baumont, M. (1959) *Notice sur la vie et les travaux de Lucien Febvre*.

Beik, W. (1985) *Absolutism and Society in Seventeenth-Century France: State Power and Provincial Aristocracy in Languedoc*, Cambridge.

Bennassar, B. (1967) *Valladolid au siècle d'or*, The Hague.

Bercé, Y.-M. (1974) *Histoire des Croquants*, Geneva (abbreviated English trans.: *The History of Peasant Revolts*, Cambridge 1990).

Besançon; A. (1968) 'Psychoanalysis, Auxiliary Science or Historical Method?', *Journal of Contemporary History*, 3, 149–62.

Besançon, A. (1971) *Histoire et expérience du moi*.

Birnbaum, N. (1978) 'The Annales School and Social Theory', *Review*, 1, 225–35.

Bloch, M. (1913) *L'Ille de France* (English trans.: *The Ille de France*, London 1971).

Bloch, M. (1924) *Les rois thaumaturges* (new edn, Paris 1983; English trans.: *The Royal Touch*, London 1973).

Bloch, M. (1925) 'Mémoire collective', *Revue de Synthèse Historique*, 40, 73–83.

Bloch, M. (1928) 'A Contribution towards a Comparative History of European Societies', in Bloch (1967), pp. 44–76.

Bloch, M. (1931) *Les caractères originaux de l'histoire rurale française* (new edn, Paris 1952; English trans.: *French Rural History*, London 1966).

Bloch, M. (1939–40) *La société feodale* (new edn, 1968; English trans.: *Feudal Society*, London 1961).

Bloch, M. (1946) *L'étrange défaite* (English trans.: *Strange Defeat*, London 1949).

Bloch, M. (1948) 'Technical Change as a Problem of Collective Psychology', *Journal of Normal and Pathological Psychology*, 104–15, reprinted in Bloch (1967), pp. 124–35.

Bloch, M. (1949) *Apologie pour l'histoire* (English trans.: *The Historian's Craft*, Manchester 1954).

Bloch, M. (1967) *Land and Work in Medieval Europe*, London (eight essays).

Blok, A. (1981) 'Rams and Billy-Goats: A Key to the Mediterranean Code of honour', *Man*, 16, 427–40.

Boer, P. de (1987) *Geschiedenis als Beroep: De Professionalisering van de Geschiedbeoefening in Frankrijk (1818–1914)*, Nijmegen.

Bois, P. (1960) *Paysans de l'Ouest*.

Bollême, G. et al. (1965) *Livre et société dans la France du 18e siècle*, 2 vols, The Hague.

Born, K. E. (1964) 'Neue Wege der Wirtschafts- und Sozialgeschichte', *Saeculum*, 15, 298–309.

Bourdieu, P. and Passeron; J. C. (1970) *La réproduction sociale* (English trans.: *Reproduction in Education, Society and Culture*, London and Beverly Hills 1977).

Bourdieu, P. (1972) *Esquisse d'une théorie de la pratique* (English trans.: *Outline of a Theory of Practice*, Cambridge 1977).

Boyle, L. (1981) 'Montaillou Revisited', in *Pathways to Medieval Peasants*, ed. J. A. Raftis, Toronto.

Braudel, F. (1928) 'Les espagnols et l'Afrique du Nord', *Revue africaine*, 69, 184–233 and 351–410.

Braudel, F. (1949) *La Méditerranée et le monde méditerranéen à l'époque de Philippe II* (second edn, enlarged, 2 vols, 1966; English trans., 2 vols, London 1972–3).

Braudel, F. (1953a) 'Présence de Lucien Febvre', *Eventail de l'histoire vivante*, 1–16.

Braudel, F. (1953b) 'Georges Gurvitch et la discontinuité du social', *Annales*, 12, 347–61.

Braudel, F. (1957) 'Lucien Febvre et l'histoire', *Cahiers internationaux de sociologie*, 22, 15–20.

Braudel, F. (1958) 'Histoire et sciences sociales: la longue durée', *Annales*, 17 (English trans. in Braudel (1980)).

Braudel, F. (1967) *Civilisation matérielle et capitalisme* (second edn, revised, *Les structures du quotidien*, 1979; English trans.: *The Structures of Everyday Life*, London 1981).

Braudel, F. (1968a) 'Marc Bloch', *International Encyclopaedia of the Social Sciences*, vol. 2, pp. 92–5.

Braudel, F. (1968b) 'Lucien Febvre', *International Encyclopaedia of the Social Sciences*, vol. 5, pp. 348–50.

Braudel, F. (1969) *Ecrits sur l'histoire* (English trans.: *On History*, Chicago 1980).

Braudel, F. (1972) 'Personal Testimony', *Journal of Modern History*, 44, 448–67.

Braudel, F. (1977) *Afterthoughts on Material Civilisation*, Baltimore and London.

Braudel, F. (1978) 'En guise de conclusion', *Review*, 1, 243–54.

Braudel, F. (1979a) *Les jeux de l'échange* (English trans.: *The Wheels of Commerce*, London 1982).

Braudel, F. (1979b) *Le temps du monde* (English trans.: *The Perspective of the World*, London 1983).

Braudel, F. (1980) *On History*, Chicago.

Braudel, F. (1981) 'The Rejection of the Reformation in France', in *History and Imagination*, ed. H. Lloyd-Jones, London, pp. 72–80.

Braudel, F. (1986) *L'identité de la France: espace et histoire* (English trans.: *The Identity of France*, vol. 1, London 1988).

Brenner, R. (1976) 'Agrarian Class Structure and Economic Development in Pre-Industrial Europe', *Past and Present*, 70, 30–74.

Brunschwig, H. (1960) *Mythes et réalités de l'impérialisme coloniale française* (English trans.: *French Imperialism*, London 1966).

Brunschwig, H. (1982) 'Souvenirs sur Marc Bloch', *Etudes Africaines offertes à H. Brunschwig*, pp. xiii–xvii.

Burguière, A. (1978) 'The New Annales', *Review*, 1, 195–205.

Burguière, A. (1979) 'Histoire d'une histoire', *Annales*, 34, 1347–59.

Burguière, A. (1983) 'La notion de mentalités chez M. Bloch et L. Febvre', *Revue de Synthèse*, 333–48.

Burguière, A. (ed.) (1986) *Dictionnaire des sciences historiques*.

Burke, P. (1973) 'The Development of Lucien Febvre', in Febvre (1973), pp. v–xii.

Burke, P. (1978) 'Reflections on the Historical Revolution in France', *Review*, 1, 147–56.

Burke, P. (1980) 'Fernand Braudel', in *The Historian at Work*, ed. J. Cannon, London, pp. 188–202.

Burke, P. (1981) 'Material Civilisation in the Work of Fernand Braudel', *Itinerario*, 5, 37–43.

Burke, P. (1986) 'Strengths and Weaknesses of the History of Mentalities', *History of European Ideas*, 7, 439–51.

Burke, P. (1988) 'Ranke the Reactionary', *Syracuse Scholar*, 9, 25–30.

Burrows, R. (1981–2) 'J. Michelet and the Annales School', *Clio*, 12, 67–81.

Buttimer, A. (1971) *Society and Milieu in the French Geographic Tradition*, Chicago.

Carbonell, C. O. (1976) *Histoire et historiens*, Toulouse.

Carbonell, C. O. and Livet, G. (eds) (1983) *Au berceau des Annales*, Toulouse.

Cedronio, M. et al. (eds) (1977) *La storiografia francese*.

Charle, C. and Delangle, C. (eds) (1987) 'La campagne électorale de Lucien Febvre au Collège de France', *Histoire de l'Education*, 34, 49–70.

Chartier, R. (1987) *Lectures et lecteurs dans l'ancien régime* (English trans.: *The Cultural Uses of Print in Early Modern France*, Princeton 1988).

Chartier, R. (1988) *Cultural History*, Cambridge.

Chartier, R. and Revel, J. (1979) 'Lucien Febvre et les sciences sociales', *Historiens et géographes*, 427–42.

Chartier et al. (1976) *L'éducation en France du 16e au 18e siècle*.

Chaunu, P. and H. (1955–60) *Séville et l'Atlantique*, 12 vols.

Chaunu, P. (1964) *L'Amérique et les Amériques*.

Chaunu, P. (1970) 'L'histoire sérielle', *Revue Historique*, 243, reprinted in Chaunu (1978a), pp. 20–7.

Chaunu, P. (1973) 'Un nouveaù champ pour l'histoire sérielle: le quantitatif au 3e niveau', *Mélanges Braudel*, Toulouse, reprinted in Chaunu (1978a), pp. 216–30.

Chaunu, P. (1978) *Histoire quantitative, histoire sérielle*.

Chaunu, P. et al. (1978) *La mort à Paris*.

Chaunu, P. (1987) 'Le fils de la morte', in Nora (1987), pp. 61–107.

Chiffoleau, J. (1980) *La comptabilité de l'au-delà*, Rome.

Chirac, D. (1984) 'The Social and Historical Landscape of Marc Bloch', in *Vision and Method in Social Science*, ed. T. Skocpol, Cambridge, ch. 2.

Clarence-Smith, W. G. (1977) 'For Braudel', *History of Africa*, 4, 275–82.

Clark, S. (1983) 'French Historians and Early Modern Popular Culture', *P&P*, 100, 62–99.

Clark, S. (1985) 'The Annales Historians', in *The Return of Grand Theory in the Social Sciences*, ed. Q. Skinner, Cambridge, pp. 177–98.

Clark, T. N. (1973) *Prophets and Patrons*, Cambridge, Mass.

Cobb, R. (1966) 'Nous des Annales', reprinted in his *A Second Identity*, London 1969, pp. 76–83.

Coleman, D. C. (1987) *History and the Economic Past*, Oxford.

Comte, A. (1864) *Cours de philosophie positive*, vol. 5.

Corbin, A. (1975) *Archaisme et modernité en Limousin au 19e siècle*.

Corbin, A. (1982) *Le miasme et la jonquille*.

Corvisier, A. (1964) *L'armée française de la fin du 17e siècle au ministère de Choiseul: le soldat*, 2 vols.

Coutau-Bégarie, H. (1983) *Le phénomène nouvelle histoire*.

Couturier, M. (1969) *Recherches sur les structures sociaux de Châteaudun 1525–1789*.

Croix, A. (1983) *La Bretagne aux 16 et 17e siècles*.

Curtius E. R. (1948) *Europäische Literatur und Lateinische Mittelalter*, Bern (English trans.: *European Literature and the Latin Middle Ages*, New York 1954).

Cvijic, J. (1918) *La péninsule balkanique*.

Darnton, R. (1978) 'The History of Mentalities', in *Structure, Consciousness and History*, ed. R. H. Brown and S. M. Lyman, Cambridge, pp. 106–36.

Darnton, R. (1984) *The Great Cat Massacre*, New York.

Davies, R. R. (1967) 'Bloch', *History*, 52, 265–86.

Davis, N. Z. (1979) 'Les conteurs de Montaillou', *Annales*, 34, 61–73.

De Certeau, M. (1975) *L'écriture de l'histoire* (English trans.: *The Writing of History*, New York 1989).

De Certeau, M. (1980) *L'invention du quotidien*.

De Certeau, M. et al. (1975) *Une politique de la langue: la Révolution française et les patois*.

Delumeau, J. (1957–9) *Vie économique et sociale de Rome dans la seconde moitié du 16e siècle*, 2 vols.

Delumeau, J. (1971) *Le Catholicisme entre Luther et Voltaire* (English trans.: *Catholicism from Luther to Voltaire*, London 1977).

Delumeau, J. (1978) *La peur en Occident*.

Delumeau, J. (1983) *Le péché et la peur.*

Devulder, C. (1985) 'Karl Lamprecht, Kulturgeschichte et histoire totale', *Revue d'Allemagne*, 17.

Deyon, P. (1967) *Amiens, capitale provinciale.*

Dion, R. (1934) *Essai sur la formation du paysage rural français*, Tours.

Dosse, F. (1987) *L'histoire en miettes.*

Dubuc, A. (1978) 'The Influence of the *Annales* School in Quebec', *Review*, 1, 123–45.

Duby, G. (1953) *La société aux 11e et 12e siècles dans la région mâconnaise.*

Duby, G. (1961) 'Histoire des mentalités', in *L'histoire et ses méthodes*, pp. 937–65.

Duby, G. (1962) *L'économie rurale et la vie des campagnes dans l'occident médiéval* (English trans.: *Rural Economy and Country Life*, London 1968).

Duby, G. (1973a) *Le dimanche de Bouvines* (English trans.: *The Legend of Bouvines*, Cambridge 1990).

Duby, G. (1974) 'Histoire sociale et idéologies des sociétés, in Le Goff and Nora (1974) (English trans. in Le Goff and Nora 1985).

Duby, G. (1978) *Les trois ordres* (English trans.: *The Three Orders*, Chicago 1980).

Duby, G. (1987) 'Le plaisir de l'historien', in Nora (1987), pp. 109–38.

Duby, G. and Lardreau, G. (1980) *Dialogues.*

Dufour, A. (1963) 'Histoire politique et psychologie historique', *Bibliothèque d'humanisme et Renaissance*, 25, 7–24.

Dumoulin, R. (1983) 'Henri Pirenne et la naissance des Annales', in Carbonell and Livet (1983), pp. 271–7.

Dumoulin, O. (1986) 'Un entrepreneur des sciences de l'homme', *Espaces-Temps*, 34–5, 31–5.

Dupront, A. (1961) 'Problèmes et méthodes d'une histoire de psychologie collective', *Annales*, 16, 3–11.

Dupront, A. (1965) 'De l'acculturation', 12th International Congress of Historical Sciences, *Rapports*, 1, 7–36.

Dupront, A. (1974) 'Religion and Religious Anthropology', in Le Goff and Nora (1974) (English version, Le Goff and Nora, 1985, ch. 6).

Dupront, A. (1987) *Du sacré.*

Durkheim, E. (1896) 'préface' to *Année Sociologique*, 1.

Erbe, M. (1979) *Zur neuereren französische Sozialforschung*, Darmstadt.

Erikson, E. (1954) *Young Man Luther*, New York.

Espace-Temps (1986) special issue on Braudel.

Evans-Pritchard, E. E. (1937) *Witchcraft, Oracles and Magic among the Azande*, Oxford.

Evans-Pritchard, E. E. (1961) 'Anthropology and History', reprinted in his *Essays in Social Anthropology*, Oxford 1962.

Farge A. (1986) *La vie fragile*.

Fauré, C. (1980) 'L'absente' (English trans.: 'Absent from History', *Signs*, 7, 1981, 71–86.

Febvre, L. (1911) *Philippe II et la Franche-Comté*, Paris.

Febvre, L. (1922) *La terre et l'évolution humaine* (English trans.: *A Geographical Introduction to History*, London 1925).

Febvre, L. (1928) *Un destin, Martin Luther* (English trans: *Martin Luther*, London 1930).

Febvre, L. (1929) 'Une question mal posée', *Revue Historique*, 30 (English trans.: Febvre (1973), pp. 44–107).

Febvre, L. (1942) *Le problème de l'incroyance au 16e siècle: la religion de Rabelais* (English trans.: *The Problem of Unbelief in the Sixteenth Century*, Cambridge, Mass. 1983).

Febvre, L. (1945) 'Souvenirs d'une grande histoire: Marc Bloch et Strasbourg', reprinted in Febvre (1953), pp. 391–407.

Febvre, L. (1953) *Combats pour l'histoire*.

Febvre, L. (1956) 'Marc Bloch', in *Architects and Craftsmen in History: Festschrift für A. P. Usher*, Tübingen, pp. 75–84.

Febvre, L. (1957) *Au coeur religieux du XVIe siècle*.

Febvre, L. (1962) *Pour une histoire à part entière*.

Febvre, L. (1973) *A New kind of History*, ed. P. Burke, London.

Febvre, L. and Martin, H.-J. (1958) *L'apparition du livre* (English trans.: *The Coming of the Book*, London 1976).

Fenlon, D. (1974) 'Encore une Question: Lucien Febvre, the Reformation and the School of *Annales*', *Historical Studies*, 9, 65–81.

Ferro, M. (1967) *La révolution russe*.

Ferro, M. (1969) *La grande guerre*.

Ferro, M. (1987) 'Des *Annales* á la nouvelle histoire', in *Philosophie et histoire*, ed. C. Descamps, Paris, pp. 37–45.

Fink, C. (1989) *Marc Bloch*, Cambridge.

Flandrin, J.-L. (1976) *Familles* (English trans.: *Families in Former Times*, Cambridge 1979).

Fleury, M. and Valmary, P. (1957) 'Les progrès de l'instruction élémentaire de Louis XIV à Napoléon III', *Population*, 72–92.

Forster, R. (1978) 'Achievements of the Annales School', *JEcH*, 38, 58–76.

Foucault, M. (1969) *L'archéologie du savoir* (English trans.: *The Order of Things*, London 1972).

François, M. (1957) 'Lucien Febvre', *Bibliothèque d'Humanisme et Renaissance*, 19, 355–8.

Frappier, J. (1969) 'Sur Lucien Febvre et son interprétation psychologique du 16e siècle', *Mélanges Lebègue*, 19–31.

Frèche, G. (1974) *Toulouse et sa région*.

Freedman, M. (1975) 'Marcel Granet', in *The Religion of the Chinese People*, ed. M. Granet, Oxford, pp. 1–29.

Furet, F. (1978) *Penser la Révolution française* (English trans.: *Interpreting the French Revolution*, Cambridge 1981).

Furet, F. (1982) *L'Atelier de l'histoire* (English trans.: *In the Workshop of History*, Chicago 1984).

Furet, F. and Halévi, R. (1989) 'L'année 1789', *Annales*, 44, 3–24.

Furet, F. and Ozouf, J. (1977) *Lire et écrire*, 2 vols (English trans. of vol. 1: *Reading and Writing*, Cambridge 1981).

Garden, M. (1970) *Lyon et les Lyonnais au 18e siècle*.

Garrett, C. (1985) 'Spirit Possession, Oral Tradition, and the Camisard Revolt', in *Popular Traditions and Learned Culture in France*, ed. M. Bertrand, Saratoga, pp. 43–61.

Gascon, R. (1971) *Grand commerce et vie urbaine au 16e siècle*.

Geremek, B. (1986) 'Marc Bloch', *Annales*, 41, 1091–1106.

Gernet, J. (1982) *Chine et christianisme* (English trans.: *China and the Christian Impact*, Cambridge 1985).

Giddens, A. (1977) 'Durkheim's Political Sociology', reprinted in his *Studies in Social and Political Theory*, London, pp. 234–72.

Gilbert, F. (1965) 'Three 20th-century Historians', in *History*, ed. J. Higham, Englewood Cliffs, pp. 315–87.

Gil Pujol, J. (1983) *Recepción de la Escuela des Annales en la historia social anglosajona*, Madrid.

Ginzburg, C. (1965) 'Marc Bloch', *Studi medievali*, 10, 335–53.

Ginzburg, C. (1976) *Il formaggio e i verni* (English trans.: *Cheese and Worms*, London 1981).

Goffman, E. (1959) *The Presentation of Self in Everyday Life*, New York.

Goubert, P. (1960) *Beauvais et le Beauvaisis*.

Goubert, P. (1966) *Louis XIV et vingt millions de français* (English trans.: *Louis XIV and Twenty Million Frenchmen*, London 1970).

Goubert, P. (1969) *L'ancien régime*, 1: *La société* (English trans.: *The Ancien Régime*, London 1973).

Goubert, P. (1973) *L'ancien régime*, 2: *Les pouvoirs*.

Goubert, P. (1982) *La vie quotidienne des paysans français au XVIIe siècle* (English trans.: *The French Peasantry in the Seventeenth Century*, Cambridge 1986).

Granet, M. (1934) *La pensée chinoise.*

Gruzinski, S. (1988) *La colonisation de l'imaginaire* (English trans. Cambridge 1990).

Guilmartin, J. F. jr (1974) *Gunpowder and Galleys*, Cambridge.

Gunder Frank, A. (1969) *Capitalism and Underdevelopment in Latin America*, Harmondsworth (second edn 1971).

Halbwachs, M. (1925) *Les cadres sociaux de la mémoire.*

Hall, J. (1980) 'The Time of History and the History of Times', *History and Theory*, 19, 113–31.

Harding, R. (1983) 'P. Goubert's Beauvaisis', *History and Theory*, 22, 178–98.

Hasluck, F. W. (1929) *Christianity and Islam under the Sultans*, 2 vols, Oxford.

Hauser, H. (1899) *Ouvriers du temps passé.*

Hendricks, L. V. (1946) *J. H. Robinson*, New York.

Henretta, J. A. (1979) 'Social History as Lived and Written', *American Historical Review*, 84, 1293–322.

Henry, L. (1956) *Anciennes familles genevoises.*

Henry, L. and Gautier, E. (1958) *La population de Crulai.*

Herlihy, D. (1978) 'Medieval Children', in *Essays on Medieval Civilization*, ed. B. K. Lackner and K. R. Philp, Austin, pp. 109–31.

Hess, A. C. (1972) 'The Battle of Lepanto and its Place in European History', *Past and Present*, 57, 53–73.

Hexter, J. (1972) 'Fernand Braudel and the Monde Braudelien'; *Journal of Modern History*, 44 reprinted in his *On Historians*, Cambridge, Mass. 1979, pp. 61–145.

Himmelfarb, G. (1987) *The New History and the Old*, Cambridge, Mass.

Hobsbawm, E. (1978) 'Comments', *Review*, 1, 157–62.

Hoskins, W. G. (1955) *The Making of the English Landscape*, London.

Hoskins, W. G. (1957) *The Midland Peasant*, London.

Hughes, H. S. (1969) *The Obstructed Path*, New York.

Hunt, D. (1970) *Parents and Children in History*, New York.

Hunt, L. (1986) 'French History in the last 20 Years', *Journal of Contemporary History*, 21, 209–24.

Huppert, G. (1978) 'The Annales School before the Annales', *Review*, 1, 215–19.

Iggers, G. (1975) *New Directions in European Historiography* (revised edn, Middletown 1984).

James, S. (1984) *The Content of Social Explanation*, Cambridge.

Jaurès, J. (1901) *Histoire socialiste de la Révolution française*, 1 (new edn, 1968).

Joutard, P. and Lecuir, J. (1985) 'Robert Mandrou', in *Histoire sociale, sensibilités collectives et mentalités*, 9–20.

Julliard, J. (1974) 'La politique', in Le Goff and Nora (1974), vol. 2, pp. 229–50.

Kellner, H. (1979) 'Disorderly Conduct: Braudel's Menippean Satire', *History and Theory*, 18, 197–222.

Keylor, W. (1975) *Academy and Community*, Cambridge, Mass.

Kinser, S. (1981) 'Annaliste Paradigm? The Geohistorical Structuralism of F. Braudel', *American Historical Review*, 86, 63–105.

Klapisch, C. (1985) *Women, Family and Ritual in Renaissance Italy*, Chicago.

Kula, W. (1960) 'Histoire et économie: la longue durée', *Annales*, 15, 294–313.

Kula, W. (1962) *Economic Theory of the Feudal System* (English trans. London 1976).

Labrousse, E. (1933) *Esquisse du mouvement des prix et des revenus*.

Labrousse, E. (1944) *La crise de l'économie française*.

Labrousse, E. (1970) 'Dynamismes économiques, dynamismes sociaux, dynamismes mentaux' in *Histoire économique et sociale de la France*, ed. F. Braudel and E. Labrousse, vol. 2, pp. 693–740.

Labrousse, E. (ed.) (1973) *Ordres et classes*.

Labrousse, E. (1980) 'Entretien' [with C. Charle], *Actes de la Recherche en Science Sociale*, 32–3, 111–22.

Lacoste, Y. (1988) 'Braudel géographe', in *Lire Braudel*, 171–218.

Lafaye, J. (1974) *Quetzlcoatl et Guadalupe* (English trans.: *Quetzlcoatl and Guadalupe*, Chicago 1976).

Lamprecht, K. (1894) *Deutsche Geschichte*, Leipzig.

Lamprecht, K. (1904) *Moderne Geschichtswissenschaft*, Leipzig.

Landes, D. (1950) 'The Statistical Study of French Crises', *Journal of Economic History*, 10, 195–211.

Langlois, C. and Seignebos, C. (1897) *Introduction aux études historiques*.

Lapeyre, H. (1955) *Une famille de marchands: les Ruiz*.

Lavisse, E. (ed.) (1900–12) *Histoire de France*, 10 vols.

Le Bras, G. (1931) 'Statistique et histoire religieuse', reprinted in his *Etudes de sociologie religieuse* (2 vols, Paris 1955–6).

Lebrun, F. (1971) *Les hommes et la mort en Anjou.*

Lefebvre, G. (1932) *La grande peur de 1789.*

Le Goff, J. (1972) 'Is Politics still the Backbone of History?', in *Historical Studies Today*, ed. F. Gilbert and S. Graubard, New York.

Le Goff, J. (1974) 'Les mentalités', in Le Goff and Nora (1974) (English trans. in Le Goff and Nora (1985), pp. 166–80).

Le Goff, J. (1977) *Pour un autre Moyen Age* (English trans.: *Time, Work and Culture in the Middle Ages*, Chicago and London 1980).

Le Goff, J. (1981) *La naissance du purgatoire* (English trans.: *The Birth of Purgatory*, London 1984).

Le Goff, J. (1983) 'préface' to reprint of Bloch (1924), *Les rois thaumaturges.*

Le Goff, J. (1987) 'L'appétit de l'histoire', in Nora (1987), pp. 173–239.

Le Goff, J. (1989) 'Comment écrire une biographie historique aujourd'hui?' *Le débat* 54, 48–53.

Le Goff, J. and Nora, P. (eds) (1974) *Faire de l'histoire*, 3 vols (English trans. (10 essays only): *Constructing the Past*, Cambridge 1985).

Le Goff, J, et al. (eds) (1978) *La nouvelle histoire.*

Le Roy Ladurie, E. (1959) 'History and Climate' (English trans. in *Economy and Society in Early Modern Europe*, ed. P. Burke, London 1972).

Le Roy Ladurie, E. (1966) *Les paysans de Languedoc* (abbrev. English trans.: *The Peasants of Languedoc*, Urbana 1974).

Le Roy Ladurie, E. (1967) *Histoire du climat* (English trans.: *Times of Feast Times of Famine*, New York 1971).

Le Roy Ladurie, E. (1973) *Le territoire de l'historien* (English trans.: *The Territory of the Historian*, Hassocks 1979).

Le Roy Ladurie, E. (1975) *Montaillou Village Occitan* (English trans.: *Montaillou*, London 1978).

Le Roy Ladurie, E. (1978a) *Le territoire de l'historien*, vol. 2 (English trans.: *The Mind and Method of the Historian*, Brighton 1981).

Le Roy Ladurie, E. (1978b) 'A Reply', *Past and Present*, 79, 55–9.

Le Roy Ladurie, E. (1979) *Le carnaval de Romans* (English trans.: *Carnival*, London 1980).

Le Roy Ladurie, E. (1982) *Paris–Montpellier: PC – PSU 1945–63.*

Le Roy Ladurie, E. (1987) *L'Etat Royal 1460–1610.*

Leuilliot, P. (1973) 'Aux origines des Annales', *Mélanges Braudel*, 2, Toulouse, 317–24.

Lévi-Strauss, C. (1983) 'Histoire et ethnologie', *Annales*, 38, 1217–31.

Lombard, D. (1967) *Le sultanat d'Atjèh au temps d'Iskandar Muda.*

Loyn, H. (1980) 'Marc Bloch', in *The Historian at Work*, ed. J. Cannon, London, pp. 121–35.

Lukes, S. (1973) *Emile Durkheim* (second edn, Harmondsworth 1975).

Lyon, B. (1985) 'Marc Bloch: Did He Repudiate Annales History?' *Journal of Medieval History*, 11, 181–91.

Lyon, B. (1987) 'M. Bloch', *French Historical Studies*, 10, 195–207.

McManners, J. (1981) 'Death and the French Historians', in *Mirrors of Mortality*, ed. J. Whaley, London 1981, pp. 106–30.

Makkai, L. (1983) 'Ars historica: On Braudel', *Review*, 6, 435–53.

Malowist, M. (1972) *Croissance et régression en Europe*.

Mandrou, R. (1957) 'Lucien Febvre', *Revue universitaire*, 66, 3–7.

Mandrou, R. (1961) *Introduction à la France moderne* (English trans.: *Introduction to Modern France*, London 1975).

Mandrou, R. (1964) *De la culture populaire aux 17e et 18e siècles*.

Mandrou, R. (1965) *Classes et luttes de classes en France au début du 17e siècle*, Messina and Florence.

Mandrou, R. (1968) *Magistrats et sorciers en France au 17e siècle*.

Mandrou, R. (1972) 'Histoire sociale et histoire des mentalités', *La Nouvelle Critique*, 41–4.

Mandrou, R. (1977) 'Lucien Febvre et la réforme', in *Historiographie de la réforme*, ed. P. Joutard, pp. 339–51.

Mann, H. D. (1971) *Lucien Febvre*.

Mantoux, P. (1906) *La révolution industrielle*.

Marcilhacy, C. (1964) *Le diocèse d'Orléans au milieu du XIXe siècle*.

Martin, H.-J. (1969) *Livre, pouvoirs et société*.

Martin, H.-J. and Chartier, R. (eds) (1983–6) *Histoire de l'édition française*, 4 vols.

Massicote, G. (1980) *L'histoire-problème: la méthode de Lucien Febvre*.

Mastrogregori, M. (1986) 'Nota sul testo dell'Apologie pour l'histoire di Marc Bloch', *Revista di storia della storiografia moderna*, 7, 5–32.

Mastrogregori, M. (1987) *Il genio della storia: le considerazioni sulla storia di Marc Bloch e Lucien Febvre e la tradizione metodologica francese*, Turin.

Mastrogregori, M. (1989) 'Le manuscrit interrompu: *Métier d'historien* de Marc Bloch', *Annales*, 44, 147–59.

Mauro, F. (1963) *Le Brésil au 16e siècle*.

Mauro, F. (1981) 'Le temps du monde pour Fernand Braudel', *Itinerario*, 5, 45–52.

Mauss, M. (1930) 'Les civilisations', reprinted in his *Essais de sociologie*, 1971.

Meuvret, J. (1946) 'Les crises de subsistance et la démographie de la

France d'ancien régime', reprinted in his *Etudes d'histoire économique*, 1971, pp. 271–8.

Meuvret, J. (1977) *Le problème des subsistances à l'époque de Louis XIV*, 2 vols, The Hague.

Michelet, J. (1842) reprinted in his *Oeuvres*, 1974, vol. 4.

Morazé, C. (1957a) 'Lucien Febvre et l'histoire vivante', *Revue historique*, 217, 1–19.

Morazé, C. (1957b) 'Lucien Febvre', *Cahiers d'histoire mondiale*, 3, 553–7.

Morazé, C. (1957c) *Les bourgeois conquérants* (English trans.: *The Triumph of the Bourgeoisie*, London 1966).

Morineau, M. (1988) 'Civilisation matérielle', in *Lire Braudel*, 25–57.

Mousnier, R. (1964) 'Problèmes de méthode dans l'étude des structures sociales', reprinted in Mousnier, *La plume la faucille et le marteau* 1970, pp. 12–26.

Mousnier, R. (1968a) *Fureurs paysannes* (English trans.: *Peasant Uprisings*, London 1971).

Mousnier, R. (ed.) (1968b) *Problèmes de stratification sociale*.

Murra, J. et al. (eds) (1986) *Anthropological History of Andean Polities*, Cambridge.

Nora, P. (1974) 'Le retour de l'événement', in Le Goff and Nora (eds) (1974), vol. 1, pp. 210 – 28.

Nora, P. (ed.) (1986) *Les lieux de mémoire*, 2: *La nation*.

Nora, P. (ed.) (1987) *Essais d'ego-histoire*.

North, D. (1978) 'Comment', *Journal of Economic History*, 38, 77–80.

Orsi, P. L. (1983) 'La storia della mentalità in Bloch e Febvre', *Rivista di storia contemporanea*, 3, 370–95.

Ozouf, M. (1976) *La fête révolutionnaire* (English trans.: *Festivals and the French Revolution*, Cambridge, Mass. 1988).

Péguy, C.-P. (1986) 'L'univers géographique de Fernand Braudel', *Espaces–Temps*, 34–5, 77–82.

Peristiany, J. G. (ed.) (1965) *Honour and Shame: The Values of Mediterranean Society*, London.

Pérouas, L. (1964) *Le diocèse de La Rochelle de 1648 à 1724*.

Perrin, C. E. (1948) 'L'oeuvre historique de Marc Bloch', *Revue historique*, 199, 161–88.

Perrot, M. (1974) *Les ouvriers en grève*.

Peyrefitte, A. (ed.) (1946) *Rue d'Ulm* (new edn, Paris 1963).

Piganiol, A. (1923) *Recherches sur les jeux romains*, Strasbourg.

Pillorget, R. (1975) *Les mouvements insurrectionels en Provence*.

Pirenne, H. (1937) *Mahomet et Charlemagne*.

Pitt-Rivers, J. (1961) *People of the Sierra*, London.

Planhol, X. de (1972) 'Historical Geography in France', in *Progress in Historical Geography*, ed. A. R. H. Baker, Newton Abbot, pp. 29–44.

Pollock, L. (1983) *Forgotten Children: Parent–Child Relations from 1500 to 1900*, Cambridge.

Pomian, K. (1978) 'Impact of the Annales School in Eastern Europe', *Review*, 1, 101–18.

Pomian, K. (1986) 'L'heure des Annales', in Nora (1986), pp. 377–429.

Popper, K. (1935) *Logik der Forschung*, Vienna (English trans.: *The Logic of Scientific Discovery*, London 1959).

Porshnev, B. (1948) (French trans.: *Les soulèvements populaires en France avant le Fronde*, 1963).

Raftis, J. A. (1962) 'Marc Bloch's Comparative Method and the Rural History of Medieval England', *Medieval Studies*, 24, 349–68.

Ratzel, F. (1897) *Politische Geographie*, Leipzig.

Raulff, U. (1986) 'Die Annales E. S. C. und die Geschichte der Mentalitäten', in *Die Geschichtlichkeit des Seelischen*, ed. G. Jättemann, Weinheim, pp. 145–66.

Raulff, U. (1988) 'Der Streitbare Prälat. Lucien Febvre', in L. Febvre, *Das Gewissen des Historikers*, Berlin, pp. 235–51.

Redfield, R. (1930) *Tepoztlan*, Chicago.

Reid, A. (1988) *The Lands below the Winds*, New Haven.

Renouvin, P. (1971) 'E. Labrousse', in *Historians of Modern Europe*, ed. H. A. Schmitt, Baton Rouge, pp. 235–54.

Revel, J. (1978) 'The Annales: Continuities and Discontinuities', *Review*, 1, 9–18.

Revel, J. (1979) 'Les paradigmes des Annales', *Annales*, 34, 1360–76.

Revel, J. (1986) 'Febvre', in *Dictionnaire des Sciences Historiques*, ed. A. Burguière, pp. 279–82.

Rhodes, R. C. (1978) 'Emile Durkheim and the Historical Thought of Marc Bloch', *Theory and Society*, 5, 45–73.

Ricoeur, P. (1980) *The Contribution of French Historiography to the Theory of History*, Oxford.

Ricoeur, P. (1983–5) *Temps et récit*, 3 vols (English trans.: *Time and Narrative*, New York 1984–8).

Robinson, J. H. (1912) *The New History*, New York.

Roche, D. (1981) *Le peuple de Paris* (English trans.: *The People of Paris*, Leamington Spa 1987).

Roche, D. (ed.) (1982) *J.-L. Ménétra: le journal de ma vie*.

Roche, D. (1989) *La culture des apparences: une histoire du vêtement, XVIIe–XVIIIe siècle.*

Roche, D. and Chartier, R. (1974) (English trans.: 'The History of the

Book', in Le Goff and Nora (1985), pp. 198–214; see Le Goff and Nora (1974)).

Rosaldo, R. (1986) 'From the Door of his Tent: The Fieldworker and the Inquisitor', in *Writing Culture*, ed. J. Clifford and G. Marcus, Berkeley, pp. 77–97.

Sahlins, M. (1981) *Historical Metaphors and Mythical Realities*, Ann Arbor.

Sahlins, M. (1985) *Islands of History*, Chicago.

Saint-Jacob, P. de (1960) *Les paysans de la Bourgogne*, Toulouse.

Schmitt, J.-C. (ed.) (1984) 'Gestures', *History and Anthropology*, 1.

Sée, H. (1901) *Les classes rurales et le régime domanial en France au moyen âge*.

Sereni, E. (1961) *Storia del paesaggio agrario italiano*, Bari.

Sewell, W. (1967) 'M. Bloch and the Logic of Comparative History', *History and Theory*, 6, 206–18.

Siegel, M. (1983) 'Henri Berr et la Revue de Synthèse Historique', in Carbonell and Livet (1983), pp. 205–18.

Simiand, F. (1903) 'Méthode historique et sciences sociales', *Revue de Synthèse Historique*, 6, 1–22 (English trans. in *Review*, 9, 1985–6, 163–213).

Simiand, F. (1932) *Recherches anciennes et nouvelles sur le mouvement général des prix*.

Spate, O. (1979–88) *The Pacific since Magellan*, 3 vols, London and Canberra.

Spencer, H. (1861) *Essays on Education* (new edn, London 1911).

Stoianovich, T. (1976) *French Historical Method: The Annales Paradigm*, Ithaca.

Stone, L. (1965) *The Crisis of the English Aristocracy 1558–1641*, Oxford.

Stone, L. (1979) 'The Revival of Narrative', *Past and Present*, 85, 3–24.

Stuard, S. M. (1981) 'The Annales School and Feminist History', *Signs*, 7, 135–43.

Suratteau, J. R. (1983) 'Les historiens, le marxisme et la naissance des Annales', in Carbonell and Livet (1983), pp. 231–46.

Thompson, E. P. (1963) *The Making of the English Working Class*, London.

Throop, P. A. (1961) 'Lucien Febvre', in *Some Twentieth-Century Historians*, ed. S. W. Halperin, Chicago, pp. 277–98.

Trevor-Roper, H. R. (1972) 'Fernand Braudel, the Annales, and the Mediterranean', *Journal of Modern History*, 44, 468–79.

Troels-Lund, T. F. (1879–1901) *Dagligt Liv i Norden*, 14 vols, Copenhagen and Christiania.

Vansina, J. (1978a) 'For Oral Tradition (but not against Braudel)' *History in Africa*, 5, 351–6.

Vansina, J. (1978b) *The Children of Woot*, Madison.

Venturi, F. (1966) 'Jaurès historien', reprinted in his *Historiens du XXe siècle*, Geneva.

Vernant, J.-P. (1966) *Mythe et pensée chez les grecs* (English trans.: *Myth and Thought in Ancient Greece*, Brighton 1979).

Veyne, P. (1976) *Le pain et le cirque*.

Vilar, P. (1962) *La Catalogne dans l'Espagne moderne*, 3 vols.

Vovelle, M. (1973) *Piété baroque et déchristianisation*.

Vovelle, M. (1976) *L'ascension irresistible de Joseph Sec*, Aix-en-Provence.

Vovelle, M. (1982) *Idéologies et mentalités* (English trans.: *Ideologies and Mentalities*, Cambridge 1990).

Wachtel, N. (1971) *La vision des vaincus* (English trans.: *The Vision of the Vanquished*, Hassocks 1977).

Walker, L. D. (1980) 'A Note on Historical Linguistics and M. Bloch's Comparative Method', *History and Theory*, 19, 154–64.

Wallerstein, I. (1974–80) *The Modern World-System*, 2 vols, New York.

Wallerstein, I. (1988) 'L'homme de la conjoncture', in *Lire Braudel*, 7–24.

Wee, H. van der (1981) 'The Global View of Fernand Braudel', *Itinerario*, 5, 30–6.

Weintraub, K. J. (1966) *Visions of Culture*, Chicago.

Wessel, M. (1985) 'De persoonlijke factor', *script* 7, no. 4 (letters of Bloch, Febvre).

Wesseling, H. (1978) 'The Annales School and the Writing of Contemporary History', *Review*, 1, 185–94.

Wesseling, H. (1981) 'Fernand Braudel, Historian of the Longue Durée', *Itinerario*, 5, 16–29.

Wesseling, H. and Oosterhoff, J. L. (1986) 'De Annales, geschiedenis en inhoudsanalyse', *Tijdschrift voor Geschiedenis*, 99, 547–68.

Wiebe, G. (1895) *Zur Geschichte der Preisrevolution des xvi und xvii Jahrhunderts*, Leipzig.

Wootton, D. (1988) 'Lucien Febvre and the Problem of Unbelief in the Early Modern Period', *Journal of Modern History*, 60, 695–730.

Wylie, L. (1957) *Village in the Vaucluse*, Cambridge, Mass.

Index